American V-Twin Engine

Timothy Remus
Chris Maida

Published by:
Wolfgang Publications Inc.
1310 Sunny Slope Ln
Stillwater, MN 55082

First published in 2001 by Wolfgang Publications Inc., 1310 Sunny
Slope Ln, Stillwater MN 55082

ISBN number: 1-929133-04-9

Printed and bound in the USA

American V-Twin Engine

From The Publisher

As both publisher and co-author this book, I have an extra-long list of people to thank. First, my hat's off to co-author Chris Maida for lending his considerable expertise to this new American V-Twin Engine book. Without his help this huge project could never have been finished.

During the writing and photography necessary for the Evo-half of the book I relied on a long list of shops and individuals, most of them well known and with sterling reputations.

The list of "helpers and guest authors" includes Tony and the Crew at Arlen Ness Inc, as well as Don Tima and the crew at Donnie Smith Custom Cycle. Speaking of good reputations, both Zipper's and Head Quarters provided help in various forms which leaves me feeling very grateful to both Dan from Zipper's and Doug from Head Quarters, as well as the rest of the employees and crew.

Additional help and images came from Custom Chrome, Crane, S&S and Andrews Products. Tom from TP Engineering consented to an interview, as did Don Tima and Bob Yost of Yost Power Tube fame.

And while it would seem all the porting work is done on automated CNC-type machines, there are still some artists who do that work by hand. We thank Lee Wickstrom from Lee's Speedshop for walking us through a typical porting job.

Most of the layout in this book is the work of Joe Plumbo while the great cover design is by Mike Urseth. For moral support I must thank my lovely and talented wife, Mary Lanz.

Timothy Remus

Acknowledgements

Our thanks to Stamford Harley-Davidson and Buell for their tech help and Buzz Kanter for the use of his photographs. We would also like to thank Dan Fitzmaurice, Jim Lewis, and the rest of the crew at Zipper's Performance for providing lots of Twin Cam parts to photograph, as well as the hours they spent with us brainstorming about what makes Twin Cams and Evos perform well. Ditto to Bob Johnson and the guys at Johnson Engine Technologies, as well as Donny Petersen of Heavy Duty Cycles in Toronto, Canada, for his technical advice and information.

Thanks also go to Dave Fussner of Wiseco Pistons, Carolyn Goss of Andrews Products, Tom Johnson and Shane Tammi of S&S Cycles, and Paul Langley and Mike Daniels of Dynojet, for their help with specific chapters. We would also like to thank Mitchell Simchowitz for the use of his 2001 Fat Boy, which we used to do all four Twin Cam installation stories, as well as disassembling the engine for the component shots in Chapter Three.

And a very big thank you goes to Mark Fabrizi of Marquee Customs and Classics for all his help. Mark did all the Twin Cam installations for this book, sometimes meeting us at 5 a.m. to fit us into his busy schedule. Mark also opened up Mitchell's TC 88B lower end so we could photograph the parts for Chapter Three.

Chris Maida

Note: Unless the photo credit indicates otherwise, images from Section I are by Chris Maida, and those in Section II are by Tim Remus.

Introduction

Some years back there was a Wolfgang book called *Ultimate V-Twin Engine.* That book, part of the Ultimate V-Twin series, was made up almost exclusively of aftermarket engines and components. Though it was a valid book, publication occurred before the introduction of the TC engines by Harley-Davidson. We've decided to replace that book with one that covers both the TC and Evo-style engines.

So what you hold in your hands is essentially two books in one. Section One deals only with the newer TC engines while Section Two deals strictly with the older EV-style engines, including those from the aftermarket.

The intent of the book is to cover common hop up and repair techniques for both engines. Section I takes you inside the new engine, including a look at the development of the engine and some of the problems encountered with the first examples of this revolutionary V-Twin. Both Section I and Section II provide ideas, both general and specific, for getting more power from either style of engine.

In an effort to make the book as useful as possible, we've included assembly and hop up photo sequences that cover both engines, from a cam install to a complete engine assembly. One of the things that this book is not, is a service manual. Thus we recommend you also have a factory manual at your side when you tear apart that new Road King to install the S&S gear-driven cam kit.

In assembling this book we've tried to focus on real-world problems and real-world hop ups. There are no turbo or NOS kits contained here, only because that is not what most riders choose most of the time. What we *have* included are some of the new big-bore engines from the aftermarket with displacements of 120 and more cubic inches.

More than anything else we've tried to give you a good background so you can make good decisions before you buy any parts – and the ability to install those parts correctly when the time comes.

History

Development of The Twin Cam 88 and 88B

Back in March of 1998, I was a member of the *American Iron Magazine* team invited out by Harley-Davidson to see the next generation of H-D engine, the Twin Cam 88, which had the internal code name P22. That team consisted of Buzz Kanter, the publisher and owner of *American Iron Magazine*, Donny Peterson, American Iron's Techline writer and owner of Heavy Duty Cycles in Toronto, and myself, Chris Maida, the editor of American Iron. Buzz came out to cover the history and corporate

As the sign (insert) says, you're not getting in here to see the new engine without an escort. On the day of our tour there was also a complete engine on hand so we could see how the whole package looked when assembled. Kanter

slant, and take photos. Donny and I were there to take the engine apart and technically analyze and understand it. I also took the tech photos, which I ended up doing on the floor of a men's room just outside of the office where we viewed the new engine. (It was the only place up there with enough light!)

The only other people outside of The Motor Company invited into this inner sanctum, which was the Archives area in the Juneau Avenue corporate headquarters, was a team from *Cycle World*. Selected staff from these two magazines were the only ones allowed to speak with the engineers, cover the engine in depth, and show to the world Harley-Davidson's latest creation and the most radical H-D engine since the overhead valve Knucklehead (the EL) replaced the side valve flatheads back in 1936.

By the time Buzz and I arrived at the Archives room, Donny had already been there a few hours and was up to his elbows in parts. He was with the major players of the TC 88's development, who were there to help us understand what H-D had created and why. Ernest "Skip" Metz, the Manager for Big Twin Powertrain Programs, was to be one of our main teachers. Skip had been involved with the project since its inception. He was joined by Don Kieffer, the Director of the Office of Program Management, Twin Cam 88 Project Leader. Don had also been involved with the project since the first conversations with Willie G. Davidson. They were joined by Bob Kobylarz, Chief Engineer of the Powertrain division, and Don Gaedke, who was responsible for making sure that H-D dealer service personal were properly trained on the new engine. Also on hand was Bill Davidson, Manager of Motorcycle Product Development for Marketing. Bill's responsible for making sure that products offered by H-D address customer's needs and concerns. Steve Piehl, who is in charge of Media Relations, was also on hand. Steve was our way past the security guards. When Buzz and I first showed up at the front desk with our cameras and tape recorders, security told us that there was no way were we getting in there with that stuff. Steve had to meet us at the front desk and personally escort us to the Archive room where everyone was waiting.

Once the introductions were finished, Bill Davidson wanted to make a few statements before

we dove into the approximately 460 new, but familiar-looking, parts spread out on the table before us. Speaking for the group, Bill stated, "When we think of Harley-Davidson, we think about its strong history, a history we are sitting in the midst of here in the Archives. I think about my great grandfather and the guys who were on the end of the production line as they watched the 1936 EL come off the line. For me to be sitting here, talking about Harley-Davidson's future, it's a great, proud moment for me." Bill also stated that a major factor in the new engine's development was maintaining the key features that are synonymous with a Harley-Davidson engine, namely an air-cooled, push rod, 45-degree V-twin design.

Another thing we learned that day was that ever-stricter EPA (Environmental Protection Agency) regulations were one of the reasons why the new engine was designed with two chain-driven cams instead of the traditional single, pinion gear-driven cam. You see, present EPA regulations require a motorcycle to produce no more than 80 decibels.

Like kids in a candy store, we didn't know what to grab next. That's me with the case in my left hand, handing a flywheel to Bob Kobylarz, Chief Engineer of the Powertrain division. To his right is Don Gaedke, while Ernest "Skip" Metz, the Manager for Big Twin Powertrain Programs is to my left. Kanter

The gearcase area, which is where the pinion gear and camshaft live on an Evo, as well as the gear drive for the externally-mounted oil pump, produces a noticeable amount of noise when the engine is running. Though The Motor Company has tried a variety of pinion gear and camshaft combinations to quiet the gearcase noise down, it would not be able to get the noise levels low enough to meet the ever-stricter EPA requirements. The only way to do that was to drive the camshaft with a chain, which meant the gearcase area would have to be redesigned. Once that was decided, a total engine redesign was put into motion. (Chapter Two will show you the parts of the TC 88 and explain how this engine design eliminated the problems that plagued the Evo.)

As for the Twin Cam 88B, the power plant of the 2000 and later Softails, back in late 1999 I spoke with Ben Vandenhoeven, Senior Project Engineer, and John Schanz, Junior Project Designer, about how the TC 88B project came about. Ben is the Twin Cam 88B team project leader and he head-

Donny took notes the entire time we were with the engineers. I took the easy way, and brought two tape recorders. (I take lousy notes.) Kanter

ed up the individual teams that were responsible for the different aspects of the engine. As for John, he was involved early on with the vehicle concept stuff. He then took over various aspects of crankcase design. John was also the project leader for the transmission design.

The TC 88B, which had the internal reference name P22 Beta, is the result of discussions that began years ago on how to reduce the vibrations of an H-D engine. Some of the early calculation and concept work was done as far back as 1993, with some strong preliminary work on the 88B in 1994. By the time the Twin Cam 88 project was approved, there was also a Twin Cam 88B project. In fact, at the onset, it was understood that the 88B would take a while longer to develop, so from the start it was meant to be launched a year after the TC 88.

By late summer of '95, the finished engine was done. In November of that same year, the TC 88B team made a presentation to the H-D management. Shortly after the first of the following year, some of the first running prototypes were ready, with running hardware for both the vehicle and chassis ready in the early spring of 1996. John stated, "I remember taking a ride to Port Washington on the first prototypes and we froze our butts off. It was early in the year, and in Wisconsin it's still real cold in March and late February. But we didn't care because it was so cool to ride it and get out on it. We just went out and did it anyway."

By the summer of 1997, there was still a little tweaking to be done to the TC 88, which was carried over to the TC 88B program. However, the 88B project was really still in the development stages. The engineers were still checking the power-train's relationship to the frame, loads through the frame, loads through the powertrain, and a multitude of other factors.

By 1998, the Twin Cam 88 was ready to be presented to selected members of the press and running pre-production bikes were at curbside. In fact, we fired one off to hear what the new motor would sound like that March in 1998 and a few weeks later Buzz and I rode two of the bikes. The TC 88B was in the tweaking stages by then, and ready for the press in mid-1999.

According to Ben, the most difficult assembly to get right on the TC 88B was what the engineers call the chain dynamic control. The chain dynamics had to be dialed in to the point where the strain on the balance shaft bearings and chain was low enough not to cause problems. However, as anyone who has owned a chain-driven bike knows, you can't have the chain too tight because it will stretch. And you don't want it too loose because it will be flopping around and wear out the sprockets. That meant the engineers had to build a hydraulic tensioning system to even out the fluctuations in the chain's tension and provide solid chain control.

In fact, this hydraulic tensioning system is tunable via a check valve that's pressed into the tensioning system support bracket. This check valve has a certain diameter orifice, which is how the hydraulic tensioning system is tuned. The reason it took the engineers a little while to get it right is because they had to go into the engine and actually change out the valve every time they wanted to test a different size orifice. Each change required stripping the engine down, changing the valve, and putting the engine back together again. The engineers also had to hook up a lot of instrumentation and recalibrate it every time the engine was broken down.

Another glitch surfaced the first time the engineers used a regular Twin Cam oil pump in an 88B. A prototype bike was left in the basement of the Juneau building overnight. During that time, all the oil drained from the oil tank into the lower end of the engine. The next day, somebody checked the tank and saw that the oil level was low so they added a couple of quarts. When the bike was started up later on, the excess oil came out and, as John says, "We got wet hands."

The problem was that on the rubber-mounted TC 88s, the oil tank is below the engine in the bottom of the transmission, so the oil pump design didn't have to keep oil from gravity-feeding into the engine. However, on the Softails, the oil tank is above the engine's lower end, under the bike's seat. The engineers needed to come up with a way to stop oil from flowing into the engine. That's why there's a wave washer in all 2000 and later Twin Cam 88 and 88B oil pumps. This oil pump design is similar to the one used on Sportster engines, though the XL pump is gear-driven, while the TC's pump is shaft-mounted. The addition of the wave washer also improves the efficiency of the pump a

little bit. The engine's hot-idle oil pressure, which is when the engine is hot and idling, is higher than what it was in the 1999 pumps by a couple of PSI's. Confused, not to worry, we'll show you what we mean in the following chapters.

NO LEAKS ALLOWED

Though there were some leaks to the press and public about the TC 88 before its actual launch, the 88B caught everyone by surprise. In fact, a lot of people, myself included, expected a rubber-mount TC 88 in the new 2000 Softails. There were two main reasons for this. First, because this project involved a smaller group of people, it wasn't revealed to as many people in The Motor Company as the Twin Cam 88 was.

The second reason was that, seeing H-D corporate felt that confidentiality was extremely critical to its success, the highest level of management made it extremely clear that leaks would not be tolerated with the 88B engine or chassis. I guess they got their point across.

Motorcycle Product Development and Marketing Manager Bill Davidson shared some of what the Twin Cam meant to his family and The Motor Company. Kanter

Inside the Twin Cam 88

More Than Just an Extra Camshaft

As was mentioned in Chapter One, the new engine from Harley-Davidson was completely redesigned to address the flaws of the Evo, meet EPA requirements for years to come, and yet look like a traditional H-D mill. It was also an engine able to handle a lot more power than its stock 88-cubic-inch displacement would produce. In fact, the redesign of this engine is so extensive that of the approximately 460 component parts used, only about 15 are the same as those used in the Evo.

A radical departure for a tradition-bound company, the TC engines are a complete redesign from the rocker box covers (which are really covers) to the heavy duty engine/transmission interface.

The horsepower of a stock TC 88 is in the low 60s (usually about 61-62) at the rear wheel in contrast to a stock Evo, which usually produced anywhere from 45 to 50 ponies. So right off the bat, the TC 88 has, on the average, 12 to 17 more horsepower to work with. Torque is higher too, as you would expect with a larger displacement engine.

But this addition power is not the big news of the Twin Cam. People have been hopping up Evos and getting a lot more power than this for years. (The Evo section of this book will tell you how to do this.) What makes the TC 88 the most innovative H-D engine in 63 years are the engine's three major design changes.

As we stated in Chapter One, the first design change is the reason why the engine has the name Twin Cam. For the first time since the JDH back in the 1920s, there are two camshafts driving the valve-train in a Harley-Davidson engine. This was done so H-D could replace the pin-ion gear-driven camshaft with a much quieter chain arrangement. The EPA requires a motorcycle to produce no more than 80 decibels. And that's for the entire bike, not just the exhaust. The intake system, valve-train, drivetrain, and any other noise producing components of the bike all factor into the 80-decibel total.

So what makes so much noise in the camshaft assembly? All Big Twin engines built before the Twin Cam

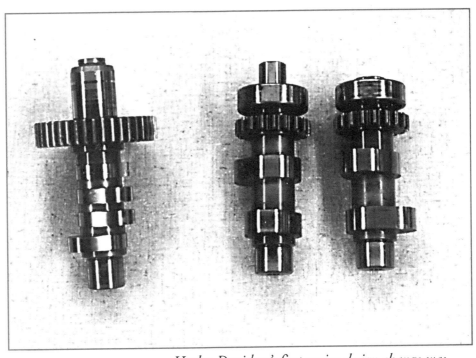

Harley-Davidson's first major design change was switching from a gear-driven cam (left) to two chain-driven camshafts (right) to reduce engine noise. Note the chain sprocket on each Twin Cam camshaft.

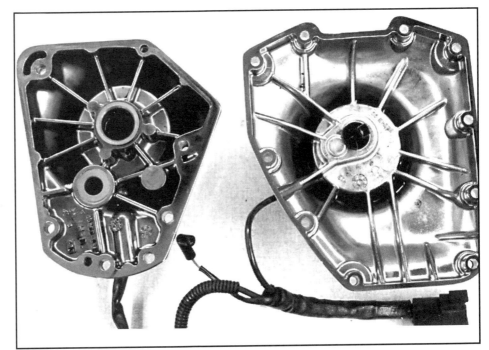

On the TC 88, covers no longer act as load bearing components. The Evo unit (left) has a bushing to support the pinion shaft and another for the camshaft. Its Twin Cam counterpart (right) is just a cover.

11

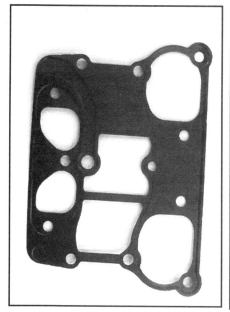

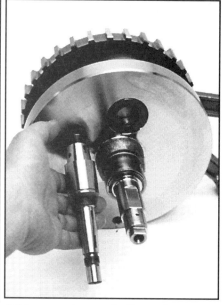

These new rocker box gaskets, which are made of embossed steel, are far superior to the paper gaskets used on Evos.

This chamber cast into the bottom of the crankcases keeps return oil off the flywheel assembly reducing parasitic drag.

This new pinion shaft, is almost 1/2" (.400") beefier than its Evo counterpart. This shaft is also a single-forging with the flywheel.

have a gear on the pinion shaf that meshes with a gear on the single camshaft. These two gears will clatter if they mesh too loosely and whine if they are too tight. Over the years, H-D has tried to make the gear-driven camshaft quieter by using an array of different size gear combinations, which succeeded to some degree. However, the steel these gears are made of will expand and contract as the engine changes temperature, which is why this has been such an ongoing headache for The Motor Company. Once the EPA announced that even tougher restrictions were on the horizon, H-D knew that the days of the gear-driven camshaft were over.

The H-D engineers decided to go with two cams because it was the best way to retain the traditional look of the H-D engine, while having the cams driven by six-plate silent chains rather than gears. If a chain went straight up from the pinion shaft to where a single cam has to be located to drive all four push rods, like the cam found in the Evo and older engines, the engine's shape would be much different than the traditional design. The powers that be at The Motor Company know that a change that drastic would never be accepted by the rank and file Harley owner. (In fact, the minor

change in appearance of the TC 88's cam cover even got a few negative remarks when I showed it to a few people back when the engine first came out.)

The most reasonable solution was to have two cams, one for each cylinder, with the first chain driven by the pinion shaft and offset from perpendicular about 22-1/2 degrees to the rear of the engine where it attaches to the rear cylinder's cam. The rear cam could then drive another six-plate silent chain, which attaches to the front cam. This way, the engine stayed very close to the traditional V-twin design and yet eliminated the gear-driven camshaft.

In fact, once the decision was made to go to two cams, the long-standing front exhaust valve ticking problem could be solved. You see, in a two cam/two cylinder engine arrangement, where each cylinder gets its own cam to operate its two valves, the rocker arms can be operated by the push rods and lifters in a much straighter line in relation to each other. This reduces the side loads, and, therefore, the wear and tear that these parts were under in earlier engines. It also means that the front cylinder exhaust valve's push rod doesn't have to reach so far forward and at a such steep angle to operate its rocker arm/exhaust valve.

The second major change incorporated into the design of the entire engine is that covers are no longer load bearing components. Covers are simply covers to hold in oil and keep out dirt. That means the rocker covers, cam (gearcase) cover, lifter blocks, and primary covers are now simply covers. These components no longer support the rocker arms, pinion shaft, camshaft, oil system breather gear, lifters, and engine and transmission. Other components and structures now support the load these parts used to bear, which results in a much quieter engine.

The most obvious result of this new design is the way the engine and transmission are bolted together. Four Grade 8 bolts now hold the two together so solidly that they appear to be one piece, like the power plant on a Sportster. This change completely eliminates any chance of flexing between the engine and tranny. In fact, the load has been taken off the primary covers so completely that the bike can be ridden without any primary covers in place and no support or structural problems would result. This new engine/transmission setup also results in better handling characteristics. With this solid connection between engine and tranny, the TC 88 can be hopped up without concerns about damaging the primary covers in high power applications.

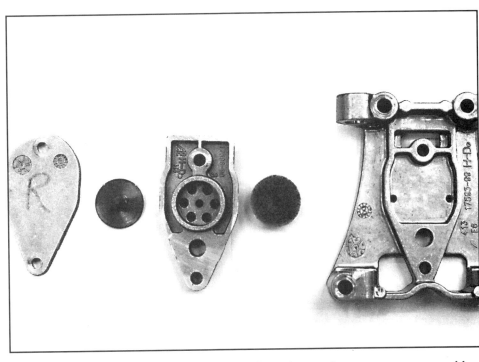

Oil spitting from the air cleaner, a common problem on Evos, is due to inefficient air/oil separation. TC 88s use this new separator so only air is sent to the air cleaner to be burned in the combustion chamber.

The body of a TC 88's connecting rods are beefier than an Evo's, and so are the wrist pin and crank pin ends.

  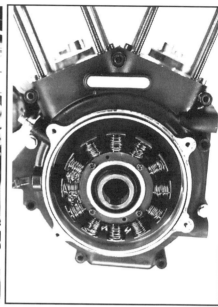

Four Grade 8 bolts connect the transmission directly to the engine which takes the load off of the primary covers.

This solid connection between the engine/transmission takes all the load off of the primary covers.

This is the left side of the engine. It's a lot like the Evo and uses the same Timken bearing, same style of alternator stator and rotor.

An outgrowth of the new engine/transmission design was a new location for the oil pump. After all, once the tranny and engine were bolted together, the oil pump couldn't stay where it has been since the days of the Knucklehead. Seeing a change was in order, the engineers decided to go to a newer style pump located inside the gearcase and driven directly by the pinion shaft. After all, why have it gear-driven again after all that work to drive the camshafts with a chain? We'll explain this new pump in more detail a little later.

The third major design change addresses three long-running problems The Motor Company has had with oil, namely leaks, air/oil separation, and parasitic drag on the flywheels. To combat oil leaks on the rocker boxes, H-D now uses high grade embossed steel core gaskets. As for the cylinder base gaskets, which were (are) a source of aggravation to many Evo owners, you'll now find O-rings where the cylinders mate with the crankcase. These new gaskets and O-rings do their job well, as we know of no chronic leaks on the TC 88 line.

The average Evo owner encounters the second problem, inefficient air/oil separation, as oil spitting out of the air cleaner housing. Here's how this comes about: Engine oil mixes with the air inside the engine. As the pistons travel up and down their respective cylinders, the flywheels that they are connected to (by the connecting rods) rotate in the oil in the lower end and throw that oil all over the inside of the crankcases and underside of the pistons. Some of this oil becomes a mist and mixes with the air in the lower end, resulting in an air/oil mist throughout the inside of the engine. Every time the pistons travel down their cylinders they increase the pressure in the engine's lower end, which has to be released to the outside or the engine's gaskets will start leaking oil. In the old days, this excessive pressure was just vented to the atmosphere through a open-ended hose from the lower end. However, that's not allowed under present EPA regulations, so the pressurized oil/air mist is channeled through some internal passageways, past an umbrella valve that is designed to allow air out but not back in, and into the air cleaner to be sucked into the engine's combustion chamber and burned during the combustion cycle. At least, that's how it is suppose to work on an Evo. However, sometimes the umbrella valve gets overwhelmed and lets oil out with the air, resulting in oil spitting (and in some cases dripping) from the air cleaner all over the right side of the engine.

On a TC 88, this pressurized oil/air mist is routed to two efficient air/oil separators (that we'll tell you about in more detail later), one located in each head, which separates the oil from the air before the air is routed to the air cleaner to be burned. Result: No more oil spitting from the air cleaner housing and no more oily air being burned in the engine causing higher than necessary exhaust emissions.

The third problem corrected by the design of the TC 88 has to do with eliminating parasitic drag on the flywheels. As stated earlier, when the flywheel assembly spins in an earlier-style H-D engine it thrashes around in oil that's pooled in the engine's lower end. Where does this oil come from? For starters, the oil that was used to lubricate the flywheel assembly drops into the crankcases after it has done its job. The rest of it is the oil that was sent to the engine's upper end to lubricate the valves, rocker arms, etc., which was returned to the engine's crankcase via oil passages in the cylinders.

This return oil is collected here on purpose because the flywheel assembly is used to transfer this oil from the crankcases to the gearcase cavity, where it is scavenged by the oil pump and returned to the oil tank. The means of transfer is simple: When the flywheels move through the oil, the oil clings to the flywheels (creating parasitic drag). In Evos and earlier Big Twins, there's an oil scrapper located on the rear wall of the crankcases, which scraps the oil from the flywheels and sends it to the gearcase area via a channel cast in the crankcases and a breather valve.

That's all changed in the TC 88s. Now return oil from the top end is dropped directly into the gearcase cavity where the oil pump is waiting to send it back to the oil reservoir. As for the pool of oil in the lower end, the oil scrapper on the rear wall of the cases has been replaced with an oil collection area in the bottom of the crankcases. This oil collection area catches all the return oil from the flywheel assembly and piston cooling oil jets (we'll tell you more about those later) and keeps excess oil off the flywheel assembly.

Now that you have an idea of how revolutionary the Twin Cam 88 series is, let's go through the entire engine and take a closer look at the components already mentioned, as well as the other parts and see how they differ from earlier designs, starting with the heart of the engine, the flywheel assembly, or crankshaft, as it is sometimes called.

THE FLYWHEEL ASSEMBLY

The left flywheel and sprocket shaft appear the same as the one used on late-model fuel-injected Evos. They are a single forging, have similar dimensions, and sport the familiar slots machined into the flywheel's outer rim so a sensor can determine flywheel speed and position for the EFI unit. The sprocket shaft Timken bearing assembly is the same as well. However, the TC 88's stroke is 4" long and shorter than the Evo's 4-1/4" stroke, which makes for a faster revving engine. The crank pin is also very different, but we'll get to that in a minute.

On the right side, the pinion shaft is part of the

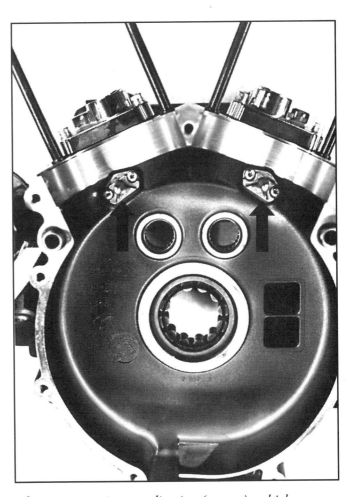

These are two piston cooling jets (arrows), which are mounted on the inside of the right crankcase. They squirt engine oil into the piston skirts and remove about 50 degrees from the piston at full load.

The new oil pump, with parts laid out. Thinner rotors on top are for the return section, while the feed uses the thicker rotors. The wave washer and the two separator plates, is in the center.

The assembled pump lives inside the gearcase cavity, eliminating any chance of an external oil leak. Here's how the rotors of the internal oil pump interlock.

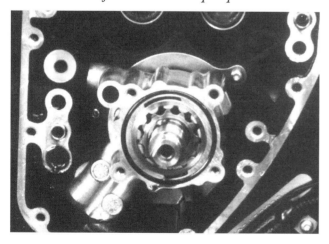

Once the pump is mounted into position in the gearcase, the pinion shaft protrudes through the two center rotors and drives them directly.

right flywheel, just like the sprocket shaft and left flywheel arrangement. However, here on the right there are some significant changes from the Evo. For one, the TC 88's pinion shaft is much beefier. In fact, it's almost 1/2" thicker (.400" to be exact), which is a major increase for a component like this. But a change of this magnitude would be pointless without a corresponding change in the pinion bearing, which supports the pinion shaft in the crankcases.

The new roller pinion bearing dwarfs its Evo counterpart. Two locating snap rings hold the pinion bearing in the right crankcase. This pinion bearing and shaft is much stronger than it needs to be for a 88" or 95" engine. In fact, this setup can handle a tremendous amount of power without being over-stressed, making it on par with the left-side Timken bearing assembly and sprocket shaft, which have never had a problem handling power on large displacement, high power Evos. The only problem on the left was on earlier engines when the sprocket shaft would spin in the flywheel in high power output engines. The chance for that to happen was eliminated when the flywheel and shaft were made as a one-piece unit.

With a lower end built like this, one would expect the connecting rods to be beefed up as well. They are. The connecting rod assembly is still the traditional configuration of a single bearing front (male) rod and a dual bearing rear (female) rod, but they are quite a bit beefier to resist being deformed under power.

The crank pin, however, is totally different. It's now almost 1/2" (.420") larger in diameter and pressed into place with a .007" interference fit. On all previous Big Twins, it was a tapered pin that was bolted to the flywheels, which would sometimes go out of true in high power applications. It's also hollow now, to save weight. That's a smart move, seeing a crank pin this size does not have to be solid to be strong enough to handle lots of power and the weight savings here will help the engine rev up quicker.

One more improvement addresses another problem of previous Big Twins, namely the single-hole crank pin. The connecting rods ride on the crank pin on three sets of roller bearings: one for the male rod and two for the forked female rod. All three of these bearing sets used to get their lubricating oil from a single oil hole located on the male rod's bearing path on earlier crank pins. This meant that the center (male rod) bearing would get the oil first and then the two outside rear rod bearings would get lubricated next. On the Twin Cam, the crank pin has three oil holes, so each bearing has its own oil supply. This is an upgrade the aftermarket has been supplying for the Evo for years and one that has proved itself to be effective in extending the life of the connecting rod bearings.

Speaking of rod bearings, these have also been upgraded. There are no longer three sets of 15 individual roller bearings in cages. There are now 18 needle rollers and they are contained in "captured" copper-coated cages. This style of cage helps break-in procedures and durability, and gives the mechanic easy wear-spot identification. Not only does each rod bearing have three more rollers than an Evo, each roller is thicker and longer than its Evo counterpart, which means a much stronger connecting rod bearing.

All this adds up to a flywheel assembly that weighs 36 pounds, which is four pounds more than a comparable Evo's at 32, but has the ability to handle much higher power levels and last much longer without a rebuild.

THE CRANKCASES

Working our way out from the flywheel assembly, we come to the TC 88's crankcases, which are split down the middle, just as they are on all Harleys. However, these new cases are made of a high-pressure, die-cast, specially-formulated, proprietary 360 aluminum alloy. And that's not the only production improvement. The entire crankcase machining process has been changed.

On the Evo, the raw crankcases had to be repositioned and clamped 32 times to be fully machined. That was a problem because every time a case is clamped down it distorts slightly, which causes slight machining distortions as the case bounces back to its original shape once it's unclamped. To produce a crankcase superior to the Evo's, the entire machining process was revamped so that a set of Twin Cam crankcases gets clamped only five times. The upgrade in material and machining results in a much better crankcase, one

that should handle high miles and/or power without a problem.

To keep excess oil off of the flywheels, as mentioned earlier, the crankcase oil scavenging area was moved from the rear portion of the cases, which is where it has been for decades, to the bottom of the crankcases.

The alternator's plug port is in about the same location as the one on an Evo, but its shape has been changed to a round opening to provide an effective seal against the elements. A magnetic sensor hole, which reads flywheel speed and position using the slots cut into the outer edge of the left flywheel, is also in this area. As for the oil pressure sending switch, it has been moved to the front of the right crankcase, near the new location for the oil filter.

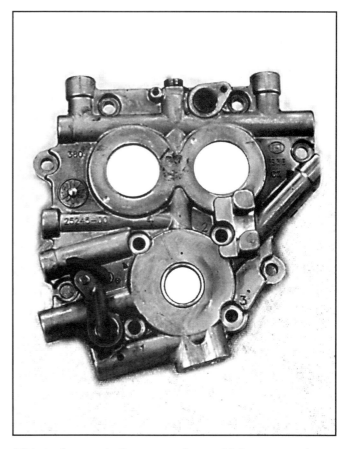

This is the camshaft support plate, which supports the outer end of the camshafts. The two top holes are for the front and rear camshaft bearings. The lower hole has a bushing to support the pinion shaft. Just above the pinion hole is another hole about .040" in diameter that sprays oil onto the chain.

Because room in the gearcase area was needed for the two chain-driven cams, the crankcase deck height, which is the area of the cases that the cylinders bolt to, was raised, making it higher than an Evo's cases. This increase in height was not a problem because the TC 88's stroke is shorter (4") than an Evo's (4-1/4"), which means the cylinders could be shorter, resulting in the same overall engine height. *In fact, a TC 88 engine and transmission unit can be bolted right into an Evo Dyna or Touring model rubber-mount frame.*

Before we leave the crankcase, there's another great change you need to know about. There are now two piston cooling jets, which we mentioned earlier, mounted on the inside of the right crankcase. These jets spray engine oil into the underside of the pistons to keep them cool.

Here's the two camshafts installed with their drive chain onto the back of the cam support plate. That's the chain tensioner at the bottom of the plate, which is actually the top of the plate.

According to The Motor Company, these jets remove about 50 degrees from the pistons at full load. Here's how they work: A spring loaded ball inside the jet allows oil to be sprayed once the oil pressure is above 16 pounds, which is at about 1500 RPM. This oil, after it cools the pistons, drops into the oil collection area in the bottom of the crankcases, to be returned to the oil pump.

THE OIL PUMP

Working our way out from the pinion bearing on the right side of the engine, we come to the new location for the oil pump, which is now driven directly by the pinion shaft, as mentioned earlier. This new pump is fully contained inside the engine's gearcase cavity, which accomplishes three important things. First, it gets it out of the way of the new transmission/engine connection. Second, it eliminates the oil pump as a source of oil leaks. Third, by having the pump driven directly by the pinion shaft instead of by a gear on the shaft, as it is in all other overhead valve Big Twins, another source of gear noise is eliminated.

This new pump is a geroter unit, which is very similar to the one The Motor Company has been using on the Sportster line since 1977 with much success. This new style pump, which uses rotors instead of gears, produces high volume and high pressure (35 psi at 2000 RPM when at operating temperature) compared to the older gear-style pump used on all previous modern Big Twins.

The pump, which is actually two pumps in one (a feed and a return), has two rotors for the feed section and two for the return. The feed section uses the thicker geroters while the thinner ones are for the return pump. One of the reasons why a gerotor pump produces better pressure and volume than a gear pump is because in a gerotor pump one rotor (the inner) moves inside its mating rotor (the outer). This allows the rotors to squeeze the oil between themselves much more effectively than the gears in an older-style pump, which are positioned side-by-side.

This new pump also uses a dual scavenge system. In the Evo and other modern Big Twins, the return oil from the engine collects in the crankcase where it is then scavenged into the gearcase cavity by means of the breather gear. Once the oil is in the gearcase, it can then be picked up by the return side of the oil pump and returned to the oil tank. On the Twin Cam, there is an oil collection area cast into the bottom of the crankcases, which collects all the return oil from the flywheel assembly and piston cooling jets. This oil collection area makes the crankcase's return oil accessible to the oil pump, which is mounted in the gearcase where it can also get to the return oil from the top end and camshaft assembly. This design allows the oil pump to scavenge oil from the crankcase and gearcase at the same time, which is why it is called a dual-scavenging pump.

THE CAMS

The next group of components that we come to on the right side of the engine is the cam assembly. Unlike on the Evo and all previous modern Big Twins, which had their single cam supported by a bearing on the right crankcase side and a bushing in the cam (gearcase) cover, the TC 88's camshafts are supported on both sides by bearings. The right crankcase side of both the front and rear cam are handled by needle bearings, which are bigger than the one used for the Evo. However, as explained earlier, the cam cover is no longer a load bearing part. It's now just a cover, which means the camshafts of the Twin Cam have to be supported by something else. That something is what the H-D engineers call the camshaft support plate. (What else?) However, due to production changes that we will discuss in Chapter Four, the other end of the front cam is supported by a ball bearing in the camshaft support plate, while the rear cam gets handled by a roller bearing.

This camshaft support plate, which bolts directly to the right crankcase, just behind the cam cover, also supports the sprockets, chains, and other components of the camshaft assembly, as well as the outer end of the pinion shaft with a bushing. The oil pump is also bolted to the cam support plate, which is used to distribute engine oil to many of the engine's components.

As for how the camshaft assembly works, the pinion shaft is the driving force for the entire camshaft/valvetrain assembly, just as it is on the Evo and all other H-D V-twins. The pinion shaft protrudes past the cam support plate so that a small sprocket can be attached to it. The rear camshaft

With the camshaft support plate installed, you can see that the rear cam protrudes through the plate, as does the pinion shaft below and to the right.

Note the chain tensioner to the left of the pinion gear and the chain guide.

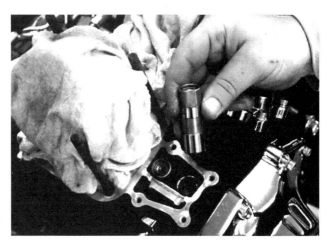

The Twin Cam's lifters have a steel body instead of a cast iron one like in Evos so they're a little more durable.

also protrudes through its bearing and past the face of the cam support plate so that another sprocket, which is twice the diameter of the one on the pinion shaft and has a Hall-effect protrusion on its face for a sensor, can be mounted onto it. These two sprockets are connected to each other by a silent chain. The rear camshaft drives the front cam with another silent chain that is located behind the cam support plate. This second chain attaches to the two cams via sprockets that are part of the two camshafts.

Everyone who has had anything that was chain-driven knows that chains, unlike gears, must be kept in proper adjustment to do their job efficiently. Both of the camshaft chains have spring-loaded tensioners, which are mounted to the cam support plate, to keep them properly adjusted. By the way, both of these silent chains have six parallel plates per link and are oiled via two tiny holes (about .040" in diameter), one per chain, in the cam support plate.

THE LIFTERS

Right above the camshafts are the four hydraulic lifters, which have also been completely changed. For starters, the lifters no longer operate inside removable lifter blocks, as they have done for decades. Keeping with the theme of covers no longer being load-bearing components, the lifters now operate inside bores in the right crankcase. The chrome covers that you see on the outside of the engine are just that, die-cast aluminum covers.

As for the lifters themselves, they have also been totally redesigned. They are now similar to the ones presently used on Sportsters and Buells, which are based on Chrysler units. These lifters also have a steel body for better wear resistance, whereas the Evo and earlier units have a cast body. Also new is how they get installed. Earlier lifters went into their bores from the bottom. These new units drop in from the top, once you remove the lifter covers, which makes changing them out a much easier task.

CYLINDERS AND HEADS

One look at how thick the TC 88's cylinders are makes an experienced mechanic think of a set of 883 Sportster cylinders, which is just what Donny Petersen and I said to each other when we saw them for the first time in the Archive room on Juneau Avenue. In fact, what we said was, "If we were gambling men, we would say it's thick enough to be bored out another 1/8", bringing the bore out to 3-7/8" for about 94 reliable cubic inches (1545cc)." Well, we were off by one inch - H-D had the 95" kit in mind when they designed the Twin Cam's steel cylinder sleeve, which is .247" (almost 1/4") thick compared to the Evo's at .173". Punching the 88" Twin Cam out to 95 inches is an easy and safe way to get a nice power gain. In fact, we show you how to do this upgrade in Chapter Seven. By the way, the stock bore of the TC 88's cylinders is 3-3/4", which is a 1/4" increase over the Evo's 3-1/2".

But boring out the cylin-

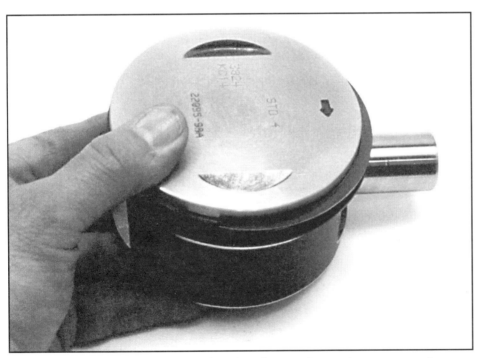

The piston, rings and wrist pin, other than being a larger diameter, are the same basic design as the Evo's, but the piston is coated with Teflon to assist with break-in skin. A directional arrow is on the piston's dome for installation purposes.

ders is not the only reason why H-D went with a sleeve this thick. The engineers also wanted a cylinder liner rigid enough not to distort under the stress of the piston's direction changes. Anyone who has taken apart many Evo top ends has seen a familiar wear pattern on the bore of the cylinder. You can see where the piston's rings have seated tight against the cylinder walls in most places, but not near where the cylinder stud holes are located. This is because the cylinder distorted a bit, resulting in the piston rings not seating tightly against the cylinder wall in those areas, which allows combustion gases to blow past the rings and into the lower end. This results in a loss of power, as well as an overly pressurized lower end and all the negatives that produces. The thickness of the TC 88's cylinders gives them the rigidity that the engineers want, even after a 95" kit is installed with its larger bore pistons.

That's not all. There are other improvements built into the TC 88's cylinders. Their cooling fins are also fatter and have more cooling fin area than an Evo's to help dissipate heat. Anyone who has ridden a Twin Cam can tell you that those fins do their job very well.

Another improvement over Evo cylinders is the new centrifugally-cast iron liner with a spiny lock surface on the outside from top to bottom. This liner is cast into the high-pressure, die-cast cylinder. Evos have a pressed-in sleeve, which would sometimes have an air gap between the sleeve and the aluminum finning, which reduced cylinder cooling. The TC 88's new liner results in a tight connection between liner and casting, which means improved heat transfer to the aluminum cylinder and its cooling fins. Also, the cylinder stud holes are made as small as possible to help with heat transfer to the cylinder fins.

As stated earlier on, when the engineers designed the TC 88 they set out to correct three major problem areas of the Evo, one of which was oil leaks and a chronic problem on the Evo was leaking cylinder base gaskets. The solution that Skip Metz and the crew came up with was O-rings, which provide a much better and longer lasting seal.

There's a groove cut into the crankcases' cylinder spigots, which is where the cylinders slide into the cases. Each cylinder has an O-ring on it that sits snugly into this groove, forming a very tight seal. There are also O-rings around two dowel locator pins, which do double duty as passageways for the oil returning from the head, through the cylinder, and into the crankcases for delivery to the gearcase cavity. These crankcase-to-cylinder surfaces and O-ring grooves are machined into the two crankcase halves when they are bolted together so a tight cylinder-to-case fit is achieved and the engine oil is kept where it belongs, inside the engine.

As for the Twin Cam heads, design-wise they are totally different than what is found on an Evo, or any other previous Big Twin. In fact, the TC 88's combustion chamber is a rounded, rectangular

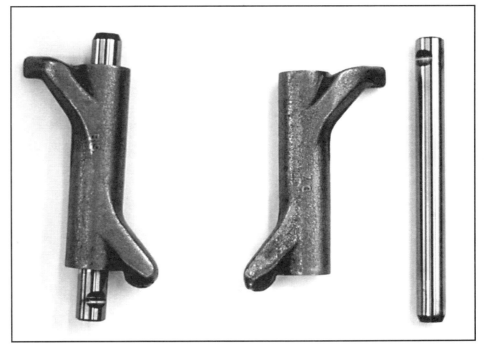

These rocker arms and rocker arm shafts are identical to an Evo's, which means all such high performance Evo parts can be used on Twin Cams.

shape, like the combustion chamber design found on early 883 Sportsters. But we won't get into the heads now. Chapter Six covers the stock TC 88 heads, as well as what is offered by the aftermarket.

THE PISTONS

The TC 88's pistons, which are shorter than an Evo's and, of course, larger in diameter, are the same basic design as the Evo's and have the standard three piston ring setup. However, these pistons are made of hypereutectic aluminum, which has a much lower expansion rate than all previous H-D pistons. This means piston-to-cylinder wall clearances can be made tighter, resulting in better performance and a quieter engine, because the pistons will stay very close to their original dimensions when at engine operating temperatures.

Because the same piston is used for both the front and rear cylinder, a directional arrow is located on the piston's crown to tell the mechanic which way to position it during assembly. These pistons also have a black Teflon coating on them from the oil ring down to ensure proper break-in.

After seeing the size of the Twin Cam's connecting rods, you may expect the piston's wrist pin to be larger than previous pins and you'd be right. An Evo wrist pin is .792" in diameter, while the TC 88's is .927", which is almost an inch in diameter and .135" larger than its Evo cousin's. The top end of the connecting rod houses a big wrist pin bushing that is capable of handling lots of power without worry.

ROCKER COVERS

As stated earlier, the new rocker boxes, which are two-piece, die-cast components and not three pieces like an Evo's, no longer support the rocker arms. The TC 88's rockers have their own separate load-bearing carrier plate, which bolts directly to the head through the bottom rocker box with four bolts. This plate, which is a high pressure die-casting, also holds the air/oil separator and breather flapper valve mentioned earlier.

These rocker boxes also have noise-dampening webbing and finning inside to help drop external noise levels. The boxes are sealed to each other and the cylinder head with the new rubber-embossed steel core gaskets mentioned earlier. These boxes are also split on an angle for easy removal when the engine is in the frame.

Here's the load-bearing carrier, which is a high pressure die-casting, with both rocker arm assemblies. Four bolts connect it directly to the head through the bottom rocker cover. The rocker assemblies are no longer supported by the rocker covers.

As for the rocker shafts and arms, they are, like the valve spring assemblies, the same as the ones used in the Evo, which means Evo high performance units will drop right in. The rocker arm geometry also remains the same as an Evo's.

THE PUSH RODS

As mentioned earlier, an advantage to having two cams is that you have a cam for each cylinder, which means the push rods are much better aligned with their respective rocker arms. That also means that new non-adjustable push rods must be used on the TC 88, though they are made from the same steel as Evo push rods. Thankfully, the two cam setup results in only two different length push rods: intakes and exhausts. The intakes are a silver color, while the push rods for the exhaust valves are black. As for the push rod tube sealing system, it's basically the same as the one used on Evos, but not exactly the same so don't try to interchange them.

LUBRICATION

The lubrication system of the Twin Cam is another area where The Motor Company has made great strides, one of which some Harley owners will be surprised to hear was not on their Evos. The TC 88 is the first H-D Big Twin to have its engine oil pass through the oil filter *before* it's sent throughout the engine. On the Evo, the oil was filtered *after* it passed through the motor. Ditto for any older Big Twin that was lucky enough to even get an oil filter.

While we're on the subject of filters, the TC 88's oil filter, which is mounted on the right side of the front of the engine cases, catches particulate as small as 10 microns, which is 10 millionths of an inch. For comparison, an Evo filter will catch particles as small as 30 microns.

After the gerotor pump pulls oil from the oil reservoir, be it an oil tank (on the Softails) or the transmission pan (Dynas and Touring models), the oil is sent into the cam support plate, which has the bypass plunger and oil pressure regulator. The cam support plate routes the oil through the crankcase to the 10-micron filter just discussed. After the filter has done its job, the now-cleaned oil is sent back through the crankcase to the cam support plate for pressurized distribution throughout the engine.

The cam support plate feeds oil to the flywheel assembly through a hole in the pinion bushing mounted in the support plate and a corresponding opening in the pinion shaft. Once the oil has lubricated the connecting rod bearings via the three oil holes in the crank pin, it drops to the bottom of the crankcase and into the oil collection area. Ditto for the oil from the piston cooling jets mention earlier.

The two outer camshaft bearings and silent chains are lubricated directly by the oil passages in the cam support plate. Once the oil has done its job, it drops to the bottom of the gearcase where it is picked up by the oil pump and returned to the oil reservoir.

Oil going to the engine's top end takes a much longer route. It first goes from the support plate to the four lifters and then travels up the push rods and into their respective rocker arms. Once the oil has passed through the rocker arms, it lubricates the valve springs and guides. Returning oil from the valve springs and guides travels down through passages in the head and into another passage in the cylinder, which is the same as what happens in an Evo. However, once the oil reaches the crankcases, it is directed into the gearcase (not the crankcase as previously discussed) where the oil pump waits to send the return oil back to its reservoir. All the other moving parts not mentioned get lubricated by splash oil or the air/oil mist that permeates the inside of the engine.

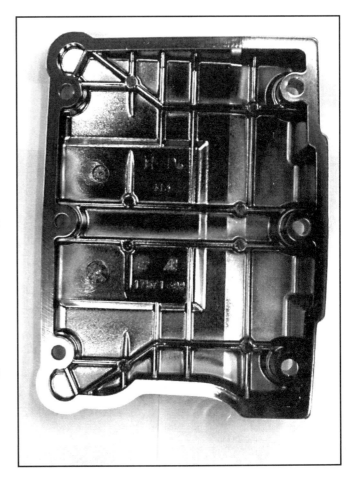

The top and bottom rocker covers are die-castings. They are strictly oil containers and cosmetic covers. The covers are split on an angle for easier removal when the engine is in the frame and have noise-absorbing webbing.

THE BREATHER SYSTEM

To eliminate the problem of oil spitting out of the air cleaner housing that would arise on some Evo engines, the H-D engineers came up with a much more effective way of separating oil droplets from the pressurized air in the engine before that air is channeled into the air cleaner to be burned during the combustion cycle. This pressurized air, which has droplets of oil in it due to the internal parts of the engine thrashing around, must now travel upward to the rocker boxes where two special air/oil separators are located in a housing that's bolted to the head through the lower rocker box. In fact, gravity helps to separate some of the oil from the air as it travels up to the rocker boxes.

Once the air/oil mist gets to the air/oil separators, it is first made to pass through a tortuous path, which allows many of the oil droplets to separate from the air and drain back down to the gearcase. The air/oil mist is then sent to a 1" long cylindric piece of open cell foam that's about 1" in diameter. This piece of foam scrubs whatever oil may still be joined to the pressurized air and lets it drain down a passageway machined into the heads for delivery to the gearcase. The now-cleaned air can then pass past a rubber, umbrella-shaped, one-way flapper valve, just like the ones found on 1992 and up Evos. These umbrella valves will let the pressurized air leave the engine via passages cast into the head near the push rod holes, into hollow breather bolts, and then into the air cleaner to be burned during the combustion cycle. However, like the Evo, these umbrella valves will not allow any air back into the engine.

FUEL DELIVERY

Seeing we're talking about the intake system, we might as well cover it now, starting with the air cleaner. The air cleaner assembly used on both the carbureted and fuel injected engines has a tapered oval shape that many people have liked more than the Evo's design. This new unit also flows more air, which is a plus for both performance and noise emissions reasons (easier airflow equals less intake noise). The air cleaner's intake port has been moved to the front of the assembly so it has access to cooler, denser air instead of heated, thinner air from around the cylinders. The engineers also redesigned the assembly's backing plate, making it flatter than the wraparound one found on the Evo to allow more air to pass over the engine's head and cylinder fins to aid in cooling.

The next component we come to is the 38.5mm CVH carburetor, which is basically the same as an Evo's, but with bigger jets to accommodate the engine's larger displacement. On engines equipped with fuel injection, the system has larger volume injectors. (We will cover the two different fuel injection systems in detail in Chapter Eight.) Idle is specified at 1000 RPM, plus or minus 50.

The intake manifold looks like an Evo's with one minor, but welcome change. The intake runners that connect to the heads are a tad longer to close the gap previously covered by the mani-

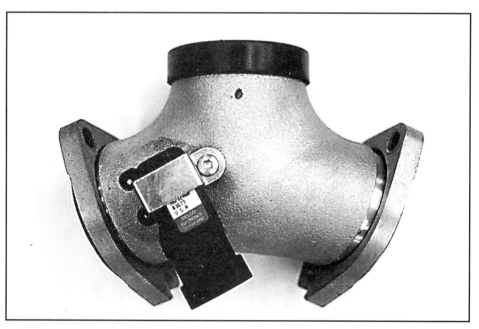

The TC 88's manifold is slightly longer than an Evo's so there's a smaller gap for the seals to fill. Though the seals look the same, they are made of Viton, which should remain pliant and resist cracking much better than the rubber used on Evo's. That black device is the ignition system's MAP sensor.

fold's rubber seals, which, by the way, are now made of Viton. This material should remain pliant and resist cracking due to high temperature a lot better than the rubber compound used on Evo seals. (Yes, you can use these new seals on your Evo manifold.) There's also a hole on the top of the manifold for a carbureted engine's ignition system MAP sensor, which we'll tell you about next.

The Ignition System

All Twin Cam 88s, both carbureted and fuel injected models, come with a single-fire ignition. Because of this, the ignition system uses a new coil, which is really two coils in one, as well as better quality spark plug wires. However, the big change over the Evo is the TC 88's use of a spark map system instead of a VOES (vacuum operated electric switch), which is basically an On/Off switch.

On the Evo, the ignition module had only two timing curves, advanced and retarded, to govern when the spark plug fired. The system's VOES, which was connected to the intake manifold via a rubber hose so it could measure the intake system's pressure, told the module when to switch between its advanced and retarded settings based on the engine's load and RPM. It worked like this: When you open the throttle a lot at a low RPM, the pressure in the intake system drops, which would make the VOES select the retarded timing curve so the engine wouldn't detonate. If you opened the throttle a lot when the engine's RPMs were high, or only a little when the RPMs were low, the manifold pressure would stay up and the advanced timing curve would control when the spark plugs fired.

The new system, however, makes changes in the ignition's timing by small increments based on its stored spark map, which is basically a chart the module (computer) reads to find out when to fire the spark plugs.

EFI models have a 16 x 16 matrix spark map, which means there are 16 boxes by 16 boxes in the chart. A carburetor-equipped engine has a 10 x 19 map. The TC 88's ignition module gets input from six main sensors, rather than just a VOES, to determine when is the best time for the spark plugs to ignite the fuel/air mixture.

These sensors measure flywheel speed and position, camshaft position, throttle position, cylinder head temperature, the fuel/air mixture charge's temperature, and barometric pressure. Carbureted models have a sensor called a MAP to measure intake manifold pressure.

Conclusion

All in all, the Twin Cam 88 is a very impressive engine, one with plenty of power for touring-minded owners, as well as the ability to handle gobs more power, if the owner is so inclined. In fact, we'll show you how to increase your TC 88's performance by boosting the displacement to 95 inches and installing hotter cams in later chapters.

As for the next chapter, we'll show you how the TC 88B, Harley-Davidson's counterbalanced engine, differs from it's rubber-mounted older brother, the TC 88.

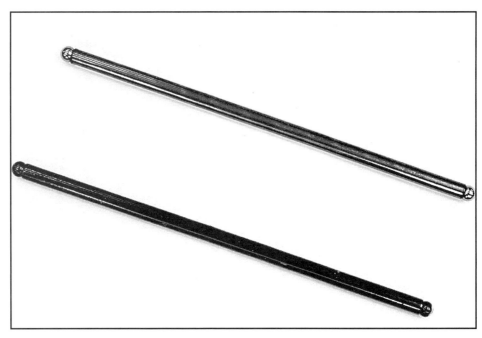

These are the new non-adjustable pushrods, silver is for intake and black is for exhaust.

The Twin Cam 88B

What makes the "B" Special

The first time the press saw the Twin Cam 88B was at the Harley-Davidson 2000 Softail model launch in Nashua, New Hampshire, in 1999. Magazine editors from all over the world had come to see what The Motor Company had in store for the Softails. Normally, H-D previews its entire new line at one showing. However, this time the Softails were being presented separately, which had everyone speculating on why they rated special treatment. Most felt that H-D had installed a rubber-

The new Softails are more than a new frame with the TC engine. They are in fact a new frame with a new counterbalanced version of the TC engine.

mounted TC 88 into a modified Softail frame, but Harley-Davidson fooled us all by unveiling the Twin Cam 88B.

Ben Vandenhoeven, the head engineer of the project, and a number of other engineers, explained the new motor, as well as The Motor Company's reason for staying with a solid-mounted engine in all the Softails models. That reason, in a word, was styling. In fact, H-D had gone to great lengths to keep the look of the Softail line as unchanged as possible in the transition from Evo to TC 88B, even though the entire machine, except for less than 20 parts (depending on model), was changed.

The powers that be at Harley-Davidson had based their decision on a survey they did of Softail owners. One of the questions asked was, "What did the owners want changed on their bikes?" The three answers most often given were more power, better acceleration, and less vibration. The H-D engineers knew that they could accomplish the first two objectives by putting the Twin Cam 88 into the Softail frame. However, the engine in a Softail has to be solid mounted or else the bike's styling will suffer, and styling was the main reason people bought Softails, according to the survey. However, The Motor Company knew that a solid-mounted TC 88 would produce more vibration than the Evo, making problem number three even worse. That meant an engine that didn't vibrate had to be invented. If you've read Chapter One, you know how that came about, so let's look at how they did it.

An Overview Of The System

The TC 88B balancing system has two counter-rotating balance shafts in the engine's lower end, which are located behind and in front of the flywheel assembly. Each balance shaft cancels out 25 percent of the engine's primary vibration, which is what makes your feet want to jump off the foot pegs at high RPMs. A bit of simple math tells you that the two balance shafts remove 50 percent. The last 50 percent is taken care of by the flywheel assembly's counterweights, which are forged right into the flywheels, as they have always been. The result of removing 100 percent of the primary vibration is a smooth-running H-D engine. However, because the Twin Cam 88B still produces

After the chain and balance shaft sprockets are positioned onto the balance shaft bracket, the bracket is bolted to the left crankcase with six Torx bolts. Once timed, the two sprockets get a washer and nut each.

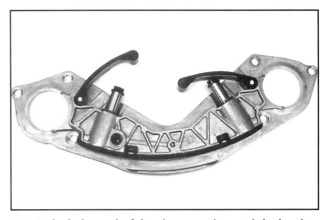

Here's the balance shaft bracket, complete with hydraulic tensioners. Note rear and front tensioner blades, which have a leaf spring inside to keep the chain under tension even when the engine is not running.

The sprockets and drive chain must be timed to the flywheel assembly. Each balance shaft sprocket has an arrow that gets aligned with its dark link on the drive chain, as does the sprocket on the pinion shaft.

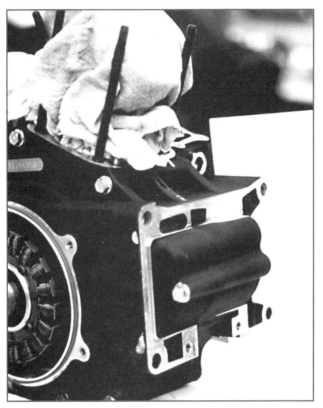

When you separate the engine and tranny, the bulge on the back of the engine becomes very apparent.

secondary vibrations, it still feels like a Harley-Davidson engine, just smoother.

Here's how the counter-rotating balance shaft system works: The two balance shafts are connected to each other and the flywheel assembly by a chain, which lives between the right flywheel and right crankcase. There's a drive sprocket on the right flywheel's (pinion) shaft. The flywheel sprocket and two balance shaft sprockets have timing marks on them that must be aligned with timing marks on the chain. If the marks are not properly set, the engine will produce primary vibration. How much depends on how far off the sprocket-to-chain timing is.

Just as with the chain-driven camshaft setup, or anything else driven by a chain, the balance shaft chain must be kept at the proper tension. To do that this system has two hydraulic chain tensioners, which are located outboard of the right flywheel. One is forward of the flywheel's shaft, while the other is aft. These tensioners use the engine's oil to keep the chain properly adjusted.

According to H-D, the balance shaft system adds 14 pounds to the weight of the engine and only causes a 1 to 1-1/2 horsepower loss at full throttle. The Motor Company also states that the system will last the life of the engine, maintenance free.

As for the top end, the TC 88B has the same heads, valves, cylinder bore, pistons, etc., as its brother, the TC 88. In fact, the 88B can use Screamin' Eagle camshafts and top end components designed for the TC 88.

Now that you know how the system works, let's check out the main components and see how they interconnect.

THE CRANKCASES

The 88B's crankcases are made of the same 360 pressure-cast aluminum that the TC 88's cases are. However, both of the 88B's case halves

The traditional front engine mount had to be abandoned in favor of a two bolt system similar to a Sportster's because the front balance shaft is where the Big Twin front mount used to be.

are not the same as the 88's in a number of ways. For starters, the 88B has a bulge at the rear and front of the crankcases to make room for the two counterrotating balance shafts. In fact, the location of the front balance shaft was the reason why the traditional front engine mount had to be abandoned.

The 88B, due to the balance shaft assembly, also has a larger crankcase volume and therefore, a larger case interface, which means it needs and has more bolts holding the two crankcase halves together. The oil collection area in the bottom of the cases is also slightly different than what you would find on the TC 88 because of the larger crankcase volume. However, the lower end is the same width as a TC 88's, though the 88B's right main (pinion) bearing is out a little further than an 88's.

The outside of the 88B's left case is the same as the TC 88's, as far as the alternator and inner primary configuration is concerned. However, on the inside it has two recesses cast into it, in the center of the crankcase bulges, to support a ball bearing for each of the two balance shafts.

The biggest change on the outside of the 88B's right crankcase, other than the bulges, is the oil filter support, which is cast into the right case. (The 88 has a separate bolt-on support

These chrome steel lines, reminiscent of the oil lines of a Knucklehead, simply pop out of their chrome fittings when released.

The right flywheel/shaft unit has a shoulder machined into it to position the drive sprocket, which is pressed onto the right (pinion) shaft. This sprocket is what drives the balance shaft assembly's chain.

On the inner face of the left case there are two recesses, one in front of the flywheel assembly and one behind, for the two balance shaft ball bearings.

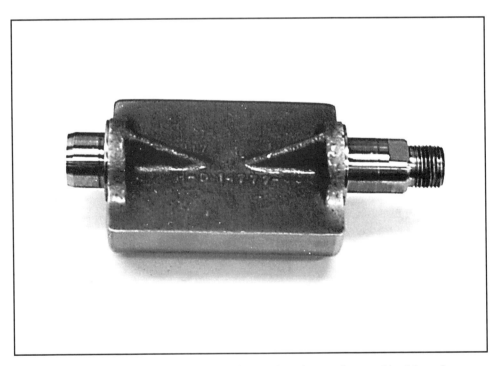

The TC 88B's two balance shafts are identical and interchangeable. Note that each one is half of a cylinder.

like the Evo, though they are not interchangeable.) There are also three quick-connect fittings mounted to the crankcase close to where the oil pump on an Evo would be. These attach to steel oil lines, reminiscent of the oil lines on a Knucklehead, which connect the 88B to its oil tank located under the seat. (The TC 88 uses rubber hoses to connect to its transmission's oil reservoir.) The movable parts of the quick-connect fittings, as well as the steel lines, use O-rings to tightly seal themselves and prevent oil leaks. The 88B's right case has a number of changes to accommodate the balance shaft assembly, such as a half shelf on the inside of the case. The right case's inner face also has two recesses cast into it for the balance shaft assembly's two hydraulic tensioners. (On the TC 88, this inner face is flush.) There's a recess in the right case for the interconnect (a rubber sleeve), which feeds oil to the hydraulic tensioners. And the opening for the right main (pinion) bearing of the flywheel assembly has also been changed because the new bearing's outside diameter is slightly narrower, but we'll get to that in a minute.

There's also an opening located just aft of the oil pump in the gearcase cavity, which feeds oil to the balance shaft assembly's hydraulic tensioners via the rubber sleeve interconnect on the inner face of the right crankcase. This opening has an oil screen in it, which is similar to the one used on the Evo for its lifters.

Lastly, the TC 88B's cases have pry slots cast into them so the mechanic can work the cases open without having to put a tool onto the crankcase's machined sealing surface.

THE FLYWHEEL ASSEMBLY

The only parts different on the TC 88B's flywheel assembly is the right flywheel/shaft unit, which sports a drive sprocket, the right (pinion) bearing race, and the pinion bearing. The left flywheel, left main bearing, crank pin, connecting rods, etc., are all TC 88 components.

The right flywheel/shaft unit has a shoulder machined into it to position the drive sprocket, which is pressed onto the right (pinion) shaft. This sprocket is what drives the balance shaft assembly's chain. The race for the right main (pinion) bearing, which is pressed onto the shaft flush against the drive sprocket, is slightly narrower than the one on the 88, as is the bearing that rides on it. This bearing is retained in the case by a semicircular plate. As for the pinion shaft, it's the same as the one found on the 88.

COUNTER-ROTATING BALANCE SHAFTS

Though the bulk of the counter-rotating balance shaft assembly is on the right side of the engine, the installation starts in the left crankcase. The first components are the two ball bearings that support the counter-rotating balance shafts. These bearings fit snugly into the two recesses cast into the left crankcase mentioned earlier. These bearings have an outside diameter of about 1-7/8" and an inside diameter of about 3/4". Once these bearings are installed in the case, the two balance shafts, which are identical solid steel units that have a machined shaft on each end, are slipped into their respective bearings.

The two balance shafts just slip into their respective bearings in the left crankcase.

Each of the two balance shaft supports have a ball bearing that is held in place by snap rings.

The two balance shaft supports, one for each balance shaft, go on next. These supports, which are not interchangeable, each have a ball bearing that slips over the right end of its balance shaft. These bearings, which are similar to, but not the same as, the ones in the left crankcase, are held in their supports by a snap ring. This snap ring helps to locate the bearings and set the endplay of the balance shafts in their bearings. The front and rear balance shaft supports, located by the bearings and dowel

The two balance shaft supports are slipped over their balance shafts and positioned into the left case by dowel pins. Note that there is a front and rear support, as noted by the F and R stamped on the support.

pins, are bolted to the left crankcase by three Torx head bolts after the balance shaft bracket is installed.

THE BALANCE SHAFT DRIVE

The balance shaft bracket rests on the ends of the balance shaft supports and is positioned by the bearings. Six 5/16" x 3-1/2" Torx head bolts, three per balance shaft support, hold the bracket and the balance shaft supports to the left crankcase. This bracket also holds the two hydraulic tensioners, as well as the rest of the balance shaft system.

The next part to go on is the plastic lower chain guide, which simply keeps the chain running along the bottom of the bracket in a smooth arc. The two tensioner blades, which are clearly marked as a front and rear unit, follow. Both of the tensioner blades have a leaf spring inside, which keeps the chain under tension even when the engine is not running. Once the engine is operating, pressurized engine oil allows the hydraulic tensioners to exert full pressure onto the chain. In addition to the leaf spring in the tensioner blades, the hydraulic tensioners themselves are spring-loaded and will apply some pressure of their own to the tensioner blades. Each ten-

The hydraulic tensioners apply pressure to the tensioner blades to keep the drive chain tight against the lower half of the flywheel assembly's drive sprocket.

32

sioner fits onto a pin that is part of the balance shaft bracket.

As for the hydraulic tensioners, though they are not as unyielding to outside pressure as a push rod lifter, the principle of operation is the same. The tensioners grow taller when filled with oil, taking up all the unwanted slack in the drive chain. The tensioners also apply pressure to the tensioner blades to keep the chain tight against the lower half of the drive sprocket, which is on the right flywheel shaft. The tensioners are designed to be more compliant than a push rod lifter so they can readily dampen fluctuations in the chain's tension.

The two balance shaft sprockets and chain go on next. An alignment pin is first put into the bottom of each balance shaft to keep them from rotating. The two sprockets, which are marked with an F for front and an R for rear, are then placed onto the balance shafts, complete with chain. The sprockets are notched so they can only go onto the balance shafts one way. The chain has dark links, which get aligned with timing arrows on the three sprockets. (Pinion sprocket arrow must aim down, while the two balance shaft sprockets point out.) This system of colored chain links and sprocket arrows properly positions the counter-rotating balance shafts to the flywheel assembly.

Once the sprockets and chain are properly positioned in the engine, the sprocket nuts and washers can be installed onto the threaded ends of the balance shafts. These nuts have high-temp thread lock on their threads to keep them in place. At this point, the right case, complete with pinion bearing, can be installed onto the flywheel assembly and left crankcase.

That wraps up the differences between the Twin Cam 88 and its brother, the Twin Cam 88B. In the next chapter we'll tell you about the teething problems the engine has gone through, what The Motor Company has done to correct the problems, as well as significant upgrades to date.

Note the plastic lower chain guide that keeps the chain running along the bottom of the bracket in a smooth arc.

Twin Cam Teething Problems

The Learning Curve

Even though the Twin Cam 88 and 88B are great engines, they have had their share of teething problems, which is nothing new in the world of technology. Though the methods of design used by modern engineers has become very sophisticated via various Computer Assisted Design (CAD) programs, unforeseen problems can and do still crop up in new engines. In fact, design flaws can even go undetected in prototype engines that are run for thousands of miles and then carefully disassembled

This shot shows the components of the old style oil pump, which is found only in 1999 engines and uses a single thick separator plate, which is sitting in Donny's left palm. Kanter

and scrutinized by engineers, as you will see.

When a flaw surfaces in a Harley-Davidson engine, an upgrade is designed and put into subsequent production engines, which (hopefully) corrects or removes the flaw. If the flaw has surfaced in enough engines, as determined by The Motor Company, a recall may go out, which will have the local dealer install the upgrade in all previously-assembled affected engines.

However, a design flaw is not the only reason why an upgrade is made in an engine design. From time to time, a better way to do something is discovered and then incorporated into current production engines. Sometimes these upgrades can be installed into previously-assembled engines, and sometimes not.

Whenever an upgrade is made, whether due to a flaw or an improvement, the new component retains the old component's part number with the addition of a letter on the end. For example, the 1999 cam support plate has the part number 25267-99, while the newest version of the plate has part number 25267-99B. The letter B shows that there have been two upgrades since the part entered service.

Now that we've covered some of the basics, let's take a look at the TC 88's teething problems and subsequent upgrades, starting with the first problem to surface: The rear camshaft and its bolt, washer, and sprocket.

Top-left is the old-style rear cam sprocket. Note that the drive key (in the center hole) is part of the sprocket. On the-right is the Andrews upgrade kit for 1999 Twin Cam 88s. Note the more pronounced keyway in the sprocket and the beefier drive key.

All 2000 and later TC 88s and 88Bs use this new style splined cam sprocket. One of the sprocket's splines is fatter than the others to properly locate the sprocket on its camshaft. Along side the gear is the cam bolt and washer for 2000 and later TC 88s and 88Bs. Note: The bolt's threads no longer go all the way to the head and the parts are much beefier than their 1999 counterparts.

THE REAR CAMSHAFT BOLT

This problem came to light early on with the production engines (those built before Sept 29, 1998, to the best of our knowledge), but never appeared on any of the test engines, which The Motor Company ran for tens of thousands of miles. This is because the glitch was part design flaw and part production problem.

The parts involved are the rear camshaft and its sprocket, which are driven by the crank (pinion) sprocket via the primary cam chain, and the bolt and washer that holds the rear camshaft sprocket onto the camshaft. As explained in Chapter Two, this assembly resides in the gearcase cavity, under the gearcase (cam) cover. And although the text in Chapter Two is about a splined camshaft and sprocket, the first version used a keyed cam.

On the keyed setup, the sprocket and drive key were formed as one piece, with the key there simply to positioning the sprocket correctly on the camshaft. A bolt and washer was to keep the sprocket and camshaft tightly together to eliminate any play between them, which would cause the key to shear. Well, that was the plan. The problem arose because the bolt was not keeping things as tight as they needed to be, so the sprocket had play on its camshaft. Result: The head of the bolt popped off, which, of course, released all load on the sprocket and allowed it to shear its key. Once this happened, the engine stopped dead in its tracks.

The reason why the sprocket was not tight to its camshaft turned out to be a collection of small glitches that added up to a big one. The first mistake was using the wrong type of bolt thread locker on the cam bolt. This caused an incorrect torque reading when the bolt was installed on the assembly line.

The second mistake involved the metal washer that goes under the head of the cam bolt. This washer was stamped out of a sheet of steel, which resulted in a not-quite-flat washer. This, in turn, resulted in an inconsistent torque load on the bolt when the engine was assembled on the production line.

Without the correct torque, whether due to one or both of these mistakes, the bolt would not be able to hold the sprocket tightly to its cam. The excessive play between these two parts sheared off the cam bolt's head and then the sprocket's key.

But why did the head of the cam bolt shear off? Well, the bolt used was threaded right up to the head. Normally, this is not a problem, but the threaded portion of a bolt is weaker than a portion without threads. So when the sprocket started wiggling on its camshaft it worked on the weak bolt until it's head finally sheared off. The sprocket's key quickly followed, which stopped the engine cold.

Once the H-D engineers figured out what was going wrong, a Service Bulletin went out and all the affected

With the bolt and washer installed in the engine, you can see how large they are in comparison to the (top) sprocket they hold on.

Design Failure Mode & Effects Analysis

In 2000, when I was interviewing Ben Vandenhoeven, the head engineer of the project, and John Schanz, Junior Project Designer, I was told that there had been a complete change in the mindset at H-D corporate. A "just good enough" approach was no longer acceptable. Everyone involved in the TC 88 and 88B project wanted to get all the bugs worked out before they launched it. In fact, John stated that, "some of the things we ran into with the TC 88 cam sprocket, for example, really turned the place upside down. It was a big issue, and a lot of focus and attention was paid to stuff like that because over the years things have changed. We're a much larger company now, and we have much better resources. So when we get little glitches like that, you truly step back and say okay, what happened here and what did we miss and how did that happen, and it helps you get better for the next time around."

In fact, according to Ben, the design teams learned a lot from the cam bolt issue and made some redesigns to the Twin Cam 88B based on that particular issue. According to Ben, "The attitude behind the rework was to identify the core problem with the cam sprocket, and the best way to get rid of the problem was to change the design to something different, something that's a lot better and has proven itself on the sprocket shaft."

One major change that it brought about at Harley-Davidson is extensive Design Failure Mode and Effects Analysis (DFMEA), which is a common practice used by the automotive industry. What happens with DFMEA is that the designers, buyers, manufacturing engineers, assemblers, and anyone else who's involved with a part sits down together and talks through the design to work out any issue or problem that these people feel they may encounter with this design.

DFMEA is basically a "what if" analysis, but a lot more structured. The participants look at a design and speculate, "What happens if this comes loose? How many times is this going to happen? How bad will it be if it does? Is it a safety issue?" If they find a high failure potential in a part, they design it out.

The same thing is done on the production end using a process called FMEA, for Failure Mode and Effects Analysis. This is when the "what if" analysis is done from the assembly side of things with questions like, "What happens if the assembler forgets to do this?"

This sort of analysis would have caught both of the problems with the camshaft sprocket and bolt issue, which was both a design weakness and an assembly line problem.

With the help of DFMEA the recall and redesign of parts like cam gears should never happen.

TC 88 engines were given an upgrade. H-D also made three changes on its assembly line. The first was to switch to a different thread locking compound; one that would not affect the bolt's torque load during assembly.

The second change was to use a different bolt; one that was not threaded right up to the head.

The last change was to the washer, which was no longer stamped out. The new washer was now ground perfectly flat to remove any chance of inconsistent torquing results.

However, while H-D was in the middle of all this, Andrews Products, which is known for its excellent camshafts and transmission gears, came out with its own fix. Andrews offers a sprocket with a separate drive key (P/N #288010), which is beefier than the cast-in key on the H-D sprocket, for all 1999 TCs.

For the 2000 models (both TC 88s and 88Bs, which were first introduced later that year), H-D completely eliminated the problem by changing the keyed rear camshaft and drive sprocket to the splined one described in Chapter Two. The camshaft bolt and washer was changed, too. They are both made much stronger now.

THE PINION BEARING

Another problem involved the new right main (pinion) bearing of the flywheel assembly, which turned out to be just a noise issue and not anything that would affect the life of the engine, although no one knew that when the noise first began to occur.

The problem was caused by air from the flywheel section of the crankcase blowing back and forth past the pinion bearing's rollers. As discussed in Chapter Two, every time the pistons travel down their cylinders they increase the pressure in the engine's lower end. Some of this pressurized air would blow past the pinion bearing's rollers and into the gearcase section of the engine. When the pistons moved back up their cylinders, the pressure in the lower end would drop, which would allow the pressurized air in the gearcase to come back into the engine's lower end, past the pinion bearing's rollers again.

This would not have been an issue if the pinion bearing's rollers were always under a load. However, there are times during the rotation of the flywheels when there's no load on some of the pinion bearing's rollers. Whenever that happened, the pressurized air blowing past the bearing's rollers would rattle the rollers against the bearing's housing. And although the rattling wasn't constant, the loading and unloading happens so fast when the engine is running that it sounded like a steady noise.

To find this one, the engineers had to check the side (axial) play between the pinion bearing's rollers and its cage, or housing. This side play measured between .006" and .022", usually. Careful checking revealed that the rattling didn't happen until the side play got to halfway

Here Donny Petersen holds an early version pinion bearing and a right flywheel.
Buzz Kanter

between .006" and .022" (about .014").

Correcting this problem was easy. H-D had the bearing manufacturer reduce the side play on all new bearings to between .002" and .008". This upgrade affected all engines manufactured after September 27, 1998, to the best of our knowledge. In fact, the pinion bearing problem, as well as the cam bolt issue, was confined to 1999 bikes.

THE PINION SHAFT

The pinion shaft was changed slightly on 2000 and later engines for both TC 88 versions. The new pinion shaft is the same size as the one found on the 1999 TC 88 models, but the depth of the slot on the section of the shaft that interfaces with the oil pump is a little bit longer to accommodate the new style oil pump we'll tell you about next.

THE OIL PUMP

All 2000 and later model TC 88s and 88Bs use the same oil pump. The 1999 TC 88s are the only ones with the (now) old-style oil pump. Knowing how much Harley mechanics love to use components and parts from other years on their bikes, the engineers at H-D state that 1999 models can not be retrofitted with the upgraded 2000 and newer oil pumps. As far as we can tell, this is due to the change in the pinion shaft just mentioned.

Though similar, the 1999 and 2000 and later pumps have a few component differences, one of which is the pump body's inner bore. On the newer pump, this inner bore is deeper than the one on a 1999 version. The new-style scavenger gerotor is also slightly thinner than the 1999 ones, which is why H-D marks 2000 gerotors with pip marks for easy identification.

The new style oil pump also has a wave washer, which is similar to, but not the same as, the one used in

Sportster oil pumps. This wave washer exerts pressure upon the parts of the pump, taking up the play between the components and stopping almost all oil flow through the pump when the engine is not running. While this was not necessary on the 1999 TC 88 because the engine's oil supply is under the transmission, the TC 88B's oil supply is in a tank that is higher than the oil pump. This means that oil could gravity feed from the tank into the engine, past the oil pump, when the engine is not running unless there is something in the pump to stop the flow. This gravity feed oil would overfill the engine's crankcases, though, unlike on previous H-D engines, the TC 88 and 88B will, upon start-up, just pump the excess oil back to the oil reservoir rather than spit it out all over itself. (That is, unless the owner added more oil to the tank before start-up thinking the oil level was low.)

The new style oil pump uses two thin separator plates instead of the single thick one used in the 1999 pump. The wave washer goes between these two separator plates.

As it turns out, an added benefit of the wave

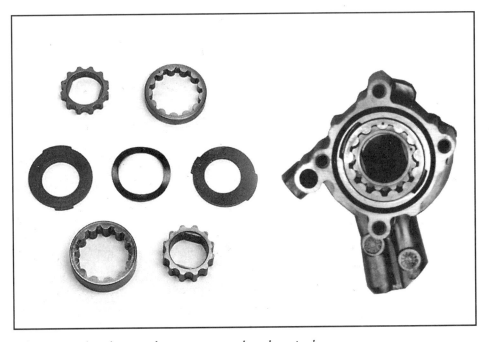

The new style oil pump has a wave washer that sits between two thin separator plates. This new pump also has pip marks on its scavenger (return) gerotors to identify them as 2000 and later units, as you can see in the assembled pump to the right.

washer is that, on the average, this pump puts out a couple pounds more pressure when at idle, at operating temperature, than the earlier pump without the wave washer. This is because, as just stated, the wave washer takes up all of the play between the pump's components, which results in a more efficient pump.

CAMSHAFT SUPPORT PLATE

Another upgrade on the 2000 engine versions was to commonize the cam support plate so that the same one could be used on both TC 88 versions. On the 88B, an oil passage from the cam support plate aligns with a passageway in the right crankcase to supply oil to the balance shaft assembly tensioners. On the TC 88, a blind boss on the right crankcase covers this support plate oil passage. The 2000 and later support plate can also be used

Looking at the back of an early 2000 commonized cam support plate, you can see the oil passage (arrow) that aligns with a passageway in the right crankcase to supply oil to the balance shaft assembly tensioners.

on 1999 engines when a screw is used to plug the passageway that the 2000 TC 88's blind boss covers on the 2000 models. The screw takes the place of the blind boss, which is not on 1999 Twin Cam right crankcases.

The camshaft support plate has also gone through other revisions since its debut in 1999, as you might have guessed from our part number example at the beginning of this chapter. The first few changes were due to problems with the rear camshaft bearing, which we'll tell you about next.

REAR CAMSHAFT BEARING

At the time of this writing, there is an ongoing issue concerning failure of the rear camshaft bearing that's mounted in the cam support plate. On some engines, this bearing gradually deteriorates until it fails completely, stopping the engine.

When this problem first surfaced, the engineers thought the fault lay with the cam support plate. Changes were made to the plate in an effort to correct the flaw, which is why there are have been a few revisions of the plate already. However, the fault turned out to be the rear ball bearing itself, or so we think.

To fix the problem, H-D changed the rear camshaft bearing on all engines assembled after mid-2000 to a roller bearing, which, so far, has not had any problems. All engines assembled before the middle of 2000 have a ball bearing supporting the rear camshaft in the support plate.

The front camshaft bearing, which is also a ball bearing, has not had any problems so far.

When a rear ball bearing is going bad, which does not always happen, it takes a while to fully let go and makes a racket under the gearcase cover until it does. In fact, an experienced mechanic can listen to the engine and usually tell if the bearing is going bad. In the event of a failure, the damage is usually confined to the gearcase and return oil system. If this happens, The Motor Company will replace all damaged parts and cover all labor charges under the owner's warranty, at no charge to the owner.

But what about owners of affected engines in which the bearing has not yet failed? What is Harley-Davidson doing for them? Well, unlike with past problems, there's presently no recall on this camshaft bearing. That means unless the bearing goes bad, Harley-Davidson will not repair the engine free of charge. What H-D has done is send owners of affected engines a letter, dated January 22, 2001, which extended the warranty on the cam bearing to five years or 50,000 miles. This warranty is also valid for future owners of the bike.

When asked about why there is no recall on the bearing, the answer given by a Harley-Davidson rep was that the number of engines that have experienced a bearing failure is less than two percent. Therefore, The Motor Company feels that it is not a widespread issue and has decided to take care of the problem if the bearing goes bad, rather than upgrade all TC 88 engines assembled before mid-2000.

What if an owner decides to upgrade to the new style bearing even if the old one has not gone bad? They can definitely do so, but it will be at his or her own expense.

If an owner plans on installing high performance cams, chain-driven, we suggest that they change over to a roller bearing for the rear camshaft when doing the job. This upgrade will not cost any extra money because both cam support plate bearings have to be changed whenever the camshafts are removed from the cam support plate anyway. By the way, we also suggest going with Torrington inner cam bearings whenever changing the camshafts, but we'll tell you all about that in Chapter Seven, which is where we show you how to install bolt-in performance camshafts.

If an owner does decide to change out the rear camshaft ball bearing for the new roller bearing, our suggestion is to do a cam upgrade at the same time. After all, you need to take the camshaft support plate assembly all apart to change the rear bearing anyway, so changing the camshafts to something with a little more umph will only increase the final bill by whatever the new camshafts cost, plus changing the inner cam bearings.

One last point, if you are thinking of also changing the front cam's ball bearing to a roller bearing, forget it. While the rear bearing's endplay can be set to the proper spec with shims, the front cam's endplay is preset to the ball bearing with a snap ring and no roller bearing presently available will exactly replace the front bearing.

CONCLUSION

As it stands right now, these are the problems and important upgrades that have occurred on the Twin Cam 88 and 88B engines. Whether or not more problems will surface, no one knows. As for upgrades, we imagine these will pop up every once in a while as The Motor Company fine tunes its latest creation.

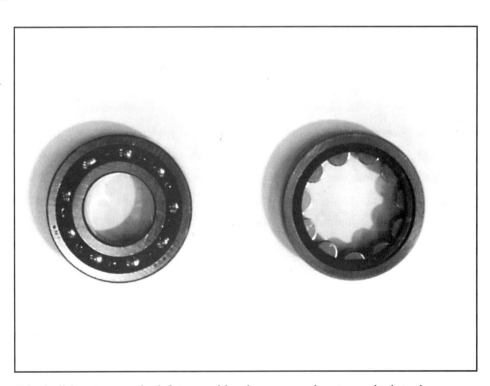

The ball bearing on the left is an old style rear cam bearing, which is the same as the present style front cam bearing. The roller bearing on the right is the new style rear cam bearing, minus its inner race.

Section I - Chapter Five

Aftermarket High Performance

The Best Ways to Get More Horses for Your TC

In their quest for more horsepower, motorcycle owners have basically three main ways to accomplish their goal. The first is to put as much fuel/air mixture over the piston as possible for the combustion event. The second is to burn the mixture in the combustion chamber as completely as possible. And the third is to get as much useful work as they can from the pressure produced by the burning fuel/air mixture. Each of these three main ways of getting more power can be accomplished by various

JIMS offers stroker and big bore kits in 106", 109", 113", and 116" displacements, which include H-beam connecting rods and pistons.

methods. Let's look at the options available for each one.

MORE DISPLACEMENT

You can get more fuel/air mixture over the piston for the combustion event by increasing the size of the cylinder's displacement via increasing the engine's cylinder bore or flywheel stroke, or both.

Increasing the engine's cylinder bore to get seven more inches of overall displacement can be accomplished in a couple of ways. As mentioned in Chapter Two, the Twin Cam's 3-3/4" bore cylinders have a very thick cylinder wall (almost 1/4"). In fact, it's thick enough to safely bore out to 3-7/8", which brings the engine's displacement up to 95". A number of companies, like Head Quarters, S&S Cycle, Screamin' Eagle, and Wiseco, make pistons for this conversion in different compression ratios. (We'll show you how to do this in Chapter Seven.)

You can also buy big bore cylinders and piston kits. Screamin' Eagle offers a 95" kit, which consists of a set of Twin Cam cylinders with a 3-7/8" bore and pistons already fitted to the cylinders. S&S and Zipper's also offer 95" big bore cylinder and piston kits. However, these three companies also have cylinders with bores that are 4" or more in size, which will increase the engine's displacement to 100" or 107", depending on the bore.

Wiseco makes pistons for the 95" conversion that you can install without having to rebalance the lower end.

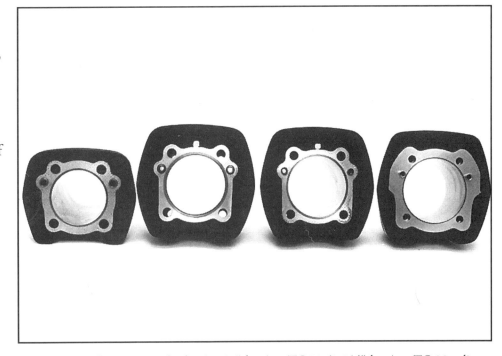

From left to right: an Evo cylinder (3-1/2" bore), a TC 88 (3-3/4" bore), a TC 88 cylinder punched out to 95" (3-7/8" bore), and Zipper's 107" cylinder (4-1/8" bore).

For example, Zipper's has a 107" Muscle Kit, which consists of 4-1/8" bore cylinders, worked heads, high compression pistons, hot cams, push rods, and a gasket kit. This kit will boost the engine's displacement out to 107", which reaps a cubic inch gain of 19 inches over the stock 88".

As for increasing the engine's stroke, which is how far the piston will travel in the cylinder bore, JIMS, S&S Cycle, and Screamin' Eagle offer various stroker kits for Twin Cam 88s. These kits come with the entire flywheel assembly, meaning both flywheels with their integral shafts, and the connecting rods, crank pin and bearings, all assembled and ready to install. Actually, they have to be. The crank pin is no longer held to the flywheels with a pair of large nuts that a local mechanic can install and remove. The TC crank pin is pressed into the flywheels with tons of pressure. These stroker kits increase the stroke of the engine from its stock 4" by moving the crank pin's location in the flywheels.

JIMS offers stroker and big bore cylinder kits that can increase a Twin Cam's displacement to 106", 109", 113", or 116", depending on which kit you use. These kits also include JIMS three-piece stroker flywheels, forged pistons, and H-beam connecting rods.

S&S also offers complete performance kits for 100", 107", and 116" engines, which include a complete flywheel assembly, heads, cylinders, pistons, carb, air cleaner, manifold, push rods, camshafts, push rod tubes, gaskets, and all hardware. They also offer many variations of this kit. You can buy a balanced system of parts, or buy the ones you want and make your own combinations.

MORE CYLINDER FILL

You can also put as much fuel/air mixture over the piston as possible for the combustion event by altering aspects of the intake and exhaust systems. By using different air cleaners, carburetors (or EFI systems, if so equipped, which we'll cover in Chapter Eight), intake manifolds, heads, valves, camshafts, and exhaust systems, you can get more fuel/air mixture into the current cylinder displacement. Let's take a look at some of your options, starting with the intake system.

There are a number of companies that make intake components, like air cleaners, carburetors, and intake manifolds. Some of the more well known carburetor suppliers are Custom Chrome (under the RevTech name), Edelbrock, Mikuni, and S&S Cycle, just to name a few. These companies, and others like them, offer carbs and other intake components to suit a variety of engine requirements.

There are also a couple of companies, like Trock Cycle and Wood Performance, that will rework your stock CVH carb so that it performs better. Then there are companies that offer kits, which will boost the carb's performance, that you can install yourself. These companies are Dynojet with its Thunderslide, and the Yost Power Tube.

As for heads and valves, we'll discuss these in depth in the next chap-

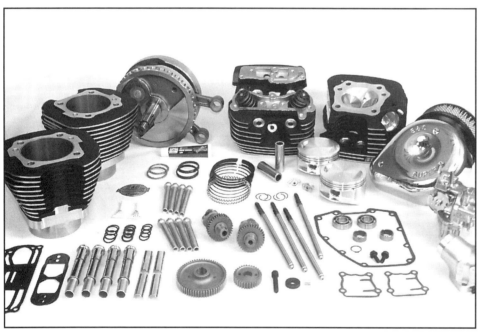

S&S offers many balanced and proven performance packages designed to give your engine the power you want. They also offer a variety of individual components.

ter. Suffice to say for now, Twin Cam head combustion chambers are much better designed than the Evo's, so extensive work is not needed in this area. However, the flow characteristics of a stock TC head's intake and exhaust ports has room for improvement.

That brings us to camshafts. As you would expect, the same companies that have offered quality cams for Evos for years, also have a selection of excellent TC cams. The more prominent manufacturers are Andrews, Crane, Head Quarters, S&S Cycle, Screamin' Eagle, and Zipper's. As with the heads, we'll deal with this subject in more depth in another chapter, namely Chapter Seven. That's when we'll show you how to install a bolt-in set of camshafts and S&S' new gear-driven camshafts.

That leaves the exhaust system, which is supplied by the same companies that offer all the Evo pipes. You can do what you want here, most people do, but remember that the pipes you install will either help or hinder the performance of your engine. While the hot ones look great, they don't always perform that way. (Some of them do work great, though.) In fact, you can have a balanced package of performance parts installed on a motor that should make it roar, and then lose a lot of potential horsepower with a poor exhaust system. One reason is because you can't get the maximum amount of fresh fuel/air mixture (or charge) into a cylinder if there's still burnt exhaust gases in it from the last combustion event. In fact, a good exhaust system not only gets all the old fumes out, it also helps draw in the next fresh charge.

Bottom line: If you are looking to increase engine performance, go with performance exhaust pipes. Our suggestion would be to buy a tunable system, like a White

Brothers e-series pipe or SuperTrapp system, especially if you plan on doing your performance upgrades over time. This way, you can keep adjusting the system to meet the engine's changing needs. Having said that, there are also a number of pipes that are not tunable, but perform great, like Cycle Shack duals, Thunderheader 2-into-1 systems, and Vance & Hines Pro-Pipes, just to name a few. Tip: If you are installing hot cams, ask one of the cam techs, which pipes they recommend.

EFFICIENT BURNS

As for the second way to get more power from your engine, a more efficient burn of the fuel/air mixture, this can also be accomplished by various methods. The first would be to have a correctly jetted and designed carburetor (or EFI system with the right maps) to provide the proper ratio of fuel and air to the combustion chamber. Too lean or too rich a mixture will not produce the most power during the combustion event.

The correct fuel/air mixture must then be thoroughly mixed via turbulence in the cylinder (caused by the shape of the piston's dome and the head's

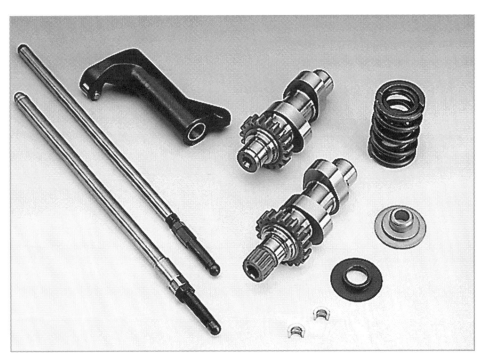

Crane Offers a variety of valvetrain components for TC 88s, like performance cams, roller rocker arms, valve spring kits, and adjustable push rods.

combustion chamber) just before it is ignited. Luckily, TC engines have excellent combustion chambers and the piston dome shapes, whether stock or from the aftermarket, are on the money, too.

With the fuel/air mixture ready to go, the ignition system's components now come into play. Use components that supply a hot, strong spark to ignite the fuel/air mixture. Crane, Compu-Fire, and Dynatek all make fully-programmable, high performance ignition system modules for the TC 88s and 88Bs. (We'll discuss the need for a fully-programmable system in a moment.) These companies also make high performance coils and wires, as does Accel and Screamin' Eagle. Just make sure the coils you choose match the ignition module you're using.

S&S offers its 4"bore cylinders for Twin Cam with or without pistons, in plain cast or black to match your engine.

Once the fuel/air mixture starts burning, the shape of the piston's dome and the head's combustion chamber must then promote excellent burning characteristics to get the most from what you have shoved in there. The Twin Cams are fine in this category, as well.

MORE COMPRESSION

The third way to increase your engine's performance is to get more useful work from the pressure produced over the piston by the burning fuel/air mixture. One method of doing this is via a higher compression ratio. This is when the fuel/air mixture is brought to a higher pressure in the combustion chamber before it is ignited. This results in more pressure pushing the piston down on its power stroke. Think of it as a coil spring. The more you can compress the spring, the harder it will push back when released.

However, there's a limit to how far you can go with this and that limit is determined by the octane of the gasoline that is available to you. Though some people would argue this point, the commonly accepted maximum compression ratio for the street is 11:1. In fact, most people who run high compression street engines have ratios of 10:1 or 10.5:1. However, if you are running a heavy bike, do not boost the engine's compression higher than 9.5:1. (As for the companies supplying high compression pistons, we named a few when discussing big bore kits earlier on.)

Octane in a fuel helps to keep it from igniting prematurely (pre-ignition) or exploding instead of burning (detonation). The textbook definition of pre-ignition is when combustion occurs in a cylinder before the spark plug has fired to ignite the fuel/air mixture. This is usually caused by hot spots in the combustion chamber. Hot spots can be caused by an overly lean fuel/air mixture or detonation. Detonation is the spontaneous, explosive combustion of the fuel/air mixture after the spark plug has ignited the fuel/air charge. Both of these are bad for your engine. In fact, excessive detonation will put holes in your pistons, as well as trash a number of other engine parts.

So how can you tell if your engine has a detonation problem? Just listen for the milkman making a delivery. By that, I mean when the engine sounds like it has milk bottles rattling around in it (this is also called *pinging*), you have a detonation problem. Immediately back off the throttle and down shift. (Don't try to power through it.) Then refill the tank with the next higher grade of fuel the first chance you get. If it still rattles, go to premium. In fact, we suggest always running premium in a performance engine, especially during the hot months of the year, or when in a urban setting where you could get stuck in traffic. An excessively hot engine is more susceptible to detonate. So is a bike that's running very lean. In fact, a hot, lean engine on a hot summer day is a prime candidate for detonation and expensive engine damage.

IGNITION ADVANCE CURVE

Another nice feature of the Twin Cam series is that you never have to set an engine's timing. It's all done by the ignition module and electronic sensors. There are only two settings you need to deal with when installing a fully-programmable module: the advance curve and rev limiter. (Leave messing with the rear cylinder's timing to the guys with the extreme machines.)

Setting the ignition's advance curve determines when the spark plug will fire to ignite the fuel/air mixture at different engine speeds (RPMs). Because the mixture must have time to burn, the spark plug actually fires before the piston reaches the top of its compression stroke, or Before Top Dead Center (BTDC). How much before (advanced) is measured in degrees of flywheel rotation, with 360 being one full rotation. Which brings us to our last method of getting more useful work from the burning fuel/air mixture: having the correct advance curve for your engine's configuration.

The right advance curve will fire the spark plug so that the pressure from the

burning gases can push its hardest down onto the piston during the power stroke. Fire the spark plug too late, and the piston has already moved too far down the cylinder to make full use of the burning mixture's pressure. Fire it too soon, and the piston is still on its way up the cylinder when the pressure starts working on it, which slows the piston's ascent to Top Dead Center (TDC). In effect, the engine is working against itself.

The problem here is that the correct advance curve is a moving target, so to speak. It can change as you change the components of the engine (compression ratio, cam duration and lift, etc.), so some trial and error testing is needed. The easiest way to tell which advance curve is the best for your particular engine is to try different settings and see what happens. This is why you need a fully-adjustable ignition module.

Start with the least aggressive advance curve setting and work your way up to the more aggressive settings. Do this by test riding the bike under full throttle operation. Does the engine ping or knock (rattle)? If not, turn off the ignition and move the advance curve up to the next setting.

Cycle Shack claims a power gain of 14.7 horsepower and 11.6 ft-lbs. on a 1999 TC 88 Dyna when Cycle Shack slip-on mufflers were used with a Mikuni HSR 42 carb and air cleaner.

S&S flywheels for Twin Cam engine come in three different strokes: 4" (the stock length), 4-1/4" (like an Evo's), and 4-5/8". Matched with a 4" piston, the displacements would be 100, 107, 116", respectively.

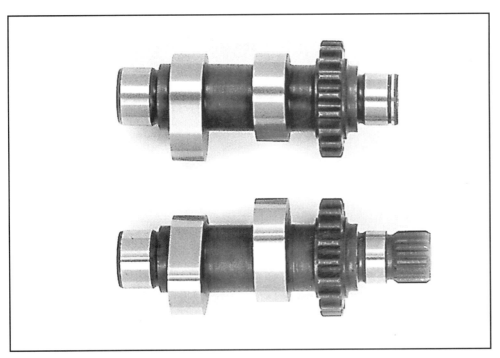

FLO Headworks cams are specially designed to be compatible with all Screamin' Eagle high performance parts and EPA-formulated pump gasoline.

Then fire it up and try again. (Note: If the engine is getting very hot, let it cool down before you continue testing.) Keep doing this until the engine rattles when you get on it hard. Then shut the engine down and turn the advance curve setting down one notch. You should now have the most aggressive advance curve the engine's present package of components can handle without causing detonation. (In fact, if you are stuck in a hot situation and the engine starts pinging, turn the advance curve down a few notches to a less aggressive setting to stop the pinging. When back in a normal riding environment, turn the advance curve back to where you had it.)

As we stated earlier, we suggest that you always run premium fuel in your high performance engine. If you have regular in it during these tests, you'll have to use a milder advance curve setting than if you ran premium. (Remember octane's job?). Also, it's not a good idea to do the tests with premium and then always put regular in the tank.

As for setting the rev limiter, we suggest setting it 500 RPM above where the horsepower curve drops off, as long as this is below the RPM limit of your valve springs. And just for the record, there's no reason to set the rev limiter above 6000 RPM in a street motor, even if the valve springs can take it. (Unless you're still making power at that RPM.)

FLAWS AND WEAK POINTS

No discussion about high performance modifications is complete without touching on the need to upgrade other parts once you have made improvements to the bike. However, we should also discuss the difference between design problems and problems that surface when high performance parts are installed.

The cam bolt and sprocket failure we discussed in Chapter Four, for example, occurred in stock engines that had never been opened for service or repair. This was clearly a design problem, one that the computer modeling did not foresee due to the reasons discussed. However, if you install a set of high lift cams and the stronger valve springs that those cams require, you may go beyond the stress levels that the engineers designed the stock parts to handle, resulting in the failure of those parts.

Problems that arise from high performance upgrades should not be blamed on The Motor Company. After all, H-D engines are designed to handle the loads and stresses imposed upon them when operating with the stock parts or those of H-D's line of Screamin' Eagle performance parts. If certain parts of the engine can not handle the stresses and loads imposed upon them by another manufacturer's parts, it's no fault of Harley-Davidson's.

We state this not to make apologies for H-D, none are needed, but to alert owners to the fact that high performance work sometimes (many times) puts other components of the bike under more stress and strain than they were originally designed for. For example, once you make the

engine produce much higher levels of power, the clutch must be beefed up to handle that additional power or it will slip. Does that mean the stock clutch is bad? No, it was not designed to handle that much power because the stock engine didn't produce it. Bottom line: As you make performance changes, be sure to give some thought as to what else may be affected by those changes and make the necessary upgrades.

With that thought in mind, remember that reputable companies in the high performance business, like the ones listed in this and other chapters, have technical support personal ready and willing to answer your questions concerning their products and what you may have to upgrade in your bike when you install their products. Make use of this service if you have any questions regarding a high performance upgrade. After all, your goal is to go faster, not break down every time you go for a ride.

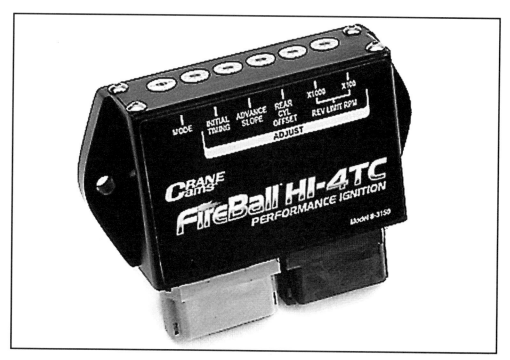

Crane's fully-programmable ignition modules for TC 88s offers a variety of settings so you can dial in the advance curve that works best with your engine's configuration.

The Twin Cam 88 Heads

Good News/Bad News

As we stated in Chapter Two, design-wise the heads of a Twin Cam are totally different than what is found on an Evo or any previous Big Twin, for that matter. However, there are some aspects of a TC's heads that are exactly the same as an Evo's,

but we'll get to those a little later. For now, let's discuss how they are different.

Place a Twin Cam head next to an Evo unit and the first thing you'll notice is the TC's fat cooling fins, which allow for much better heat dissipa-

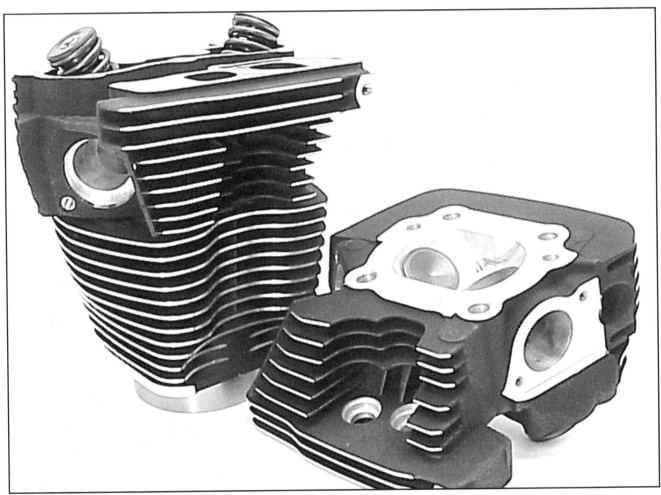

Though a Twin Cam head's design is totally different than what is found on an Evo (or any previous Big Twin), there are some aspects that are exactly that same as an Evo's. Zipper's

tion. In fact, the Twin Cam heads have about 60 percent more finning surface than an Evo's. If you doubt this finning design works, ask anyone who's ridden a TC 88 in the summer. Folks, it's just doing its job and doing it well.

There's also big changes in the combustion chamber. Stock Evos have a rounded chamber, which is cut off on one side like a D. This cut off section is flat and even with the surrounding gasket surface. When the fuel/air mixture in the cylinder is compressed into the head's combustion chamber by the flat-top piston, some of the mixture is pushed up against the flat section of the D, which "squishes" the mixture into the rounded section of the head, creating turbulence. This turbulence helps to thoroughly mix the fuel and air in the combustion chamber, which results in a more efficient burn once the mixture is ignited. This is one of the reasons why Evos run much leaner and cleaner, and produce more power than previous engine designs, such as Knuckleheads, Panheads, and Shovelheads. But though the Evo design is much better than the hemispherical combustion chambers found on these earlier engines, it has a squish area on only one side of the combustion chamber.

The bathtub chamber design of a TC 88 head, however, is more of a rounded, rectangular shape, which provides a flat squish band all around the combustion

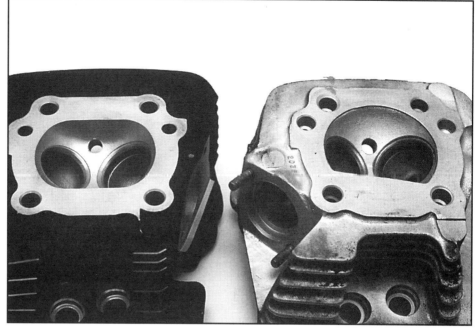

The TC's combustion chamber (left) has more of a rounded, rectangular shape, which provides a flat squish band all around the combustion chamber. The Evo's D-shape (right) allows for a squish band from one direction only.

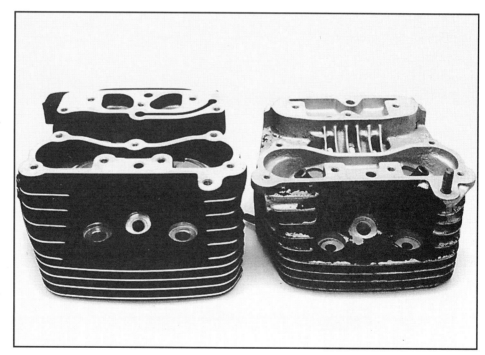

The head on the right is from an Evo, while the one on the left is for the Twin Cam. As you can see, the Twin Cam's cooling fins are much fatter, which helps the engine dissipate heat quicker.

chamber. This allows the TC 88's flat-topped pistons to compress the fuel/air mixture into the combustion chamber with more turbulence, which results in a better mixing of the fuel and air and a better burn. Result: more power with less exhaust emissions. This bathtub combustion chamber has a volume of about 85cc (we say *about* because of variances in the casting), which is about 7cc bigger than the Evo's 78cc chamber. The compression ratio on a TC 88 is also higher, about 8.9:1, than the Evo's 8.5:1.

The next change you should note is the switch from a 14mm spark plug to a smaller 12mm one. Because the bathtub combustion chamber has less room between the valve seat insert and the spark plug hole, the H-D engineers decided to go with the smaller plug, and therefore a smaller plug hole, to ensure that the plug hole would not cause a weakness in the head's casting. Dropping to the smaller plug is a smart move and does not affect how well the plug will work, but it does result in a stronger head design.

If you look at the right side of the head, you'll find a passage near the push rod holes. This pas-

sageway allows the pressurized air/oil gases, which we discussed in the second chapter, to exit the head through a hollow breather bolt and enter the air cleaner to be burned during the combustion event.

The last few changes involve the exhaust port, the diameter of which is slightly smaller than the intake. The H-D engineers stated that this was done to get higher exhaust gas velocities and, therefore, a more effective evacuation of the cylinder. There's also an anti-reversion step at the exit point of the exhaust port to keep exhaust gases already in the exhaust pipe from reentering the combustion chamber. When we talked with Dan Fitzmaurice of Zipper's, a highly regarded shop with 20 years of high performance experience, Dan stated that he believed H-D put in the anti-reversion step so that when an owner puts on a flashy, but poor performing exhaust system, the engine would still run well, though not anywhere near its performance potential.

EVO SIMILARITIES

As for the ways a TC head is like an Evo, the first is the material they are made of. Twin Cam heads are made of the same 242 aluminum alloy used to make Evo heads, which makes sense seeing there haven't been any problems with Evo heads.

The intake tract of a Twin Cam is similar to an Evo's, though they are not exactly the same. In fact, additional horsepower is hiding in some of the same spots, but we'll get to that in a moment.

As for the valves, the Twin Cam uses the same size intake valve as an Evo. However, the exhaust valve is a little thicker and about .030" smaller in diameter to match the smaller exhaust port. To make the TC 88 exhaust valve easy to identi-

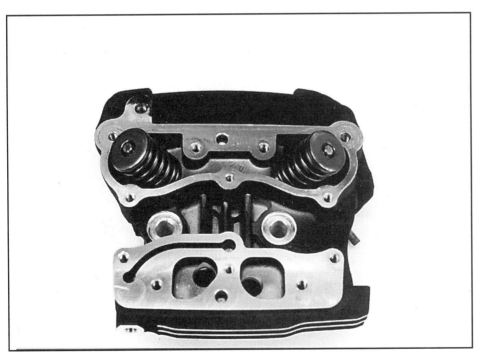

The Twin Cam's valve springs and keepers are the same as an Evo's, which means all the high performance valve spring kits produced for the Evo will also fit the TC 88 without modification.

fy, it is marked with an indent in the center of its face. In fact, even the valve angles are the same as an Evo's.

Seeing the intake valves are the same, and the exhaust valves almost so, it stands to reason that the Twin Cam's valve springs and keepers are the same as an Evo's, which they are. That means all the high performance valve spring kits produced for the Evo will also fit the TC 88 without modification. By the way, if you're thinking of swapping out the heads on your Evo for a set of TC 88 ones, forget it. The bolt pattern is bigger on the TC 88 heads to give adequate clearance for the 1/4" larger bore of the cylinders.

But as good as these heads sound, the stock heads on both versions of the Twin Cam do not flow as much air as an Evo head. Though that doesn't make sense, seeing Evo heads need to feed only a 80" engine while Twin Cam heads must supply an 88" or 95" engine, it's true.

Now, if you're not interested in getting substantially more power out of your engine, the stock heads will do the job just fine, even if you go with the 95-cubic-inch upgrade. (We'll show you how to do this in Chapter Seven.) However, if you want better performance from your TC 88 heads, you have two choices: have the stock ones reworked by a pro (forget the guy down the street with the Dremel tool), or buy a new set of heads.

Evo owners had the same decision to make, which is why there's so many experienced and qualified shops around ready and able to rework your Twin Cam's heads. Let's take reworking the heads first, then we'll list some of the companies that make new heads.

REWORKING THE HEADS

Though Twin Cam heads incorporate many improvements over an Evo's, they still have a similar intake and exhaust tract and, therefore, some of the same flow problems. That also means that some of the tricks head porters have been using on the Evo for the last 15 years to get better airflow will also work on a TC head. (We cover some of these in the Evo section.)

So how should you go about getting TC heads to breath as they should so the engine can make some real power? Dan Fitzmaurice recommends porting out the heads and then installing bigger valves. Seeing the TC has the same intake valve as an Evo, installing the same oversized valve that has been used for years in high performance Evo heads will do the job. (How big a valve depends on the engine's specifications.)

But what about the intake port? On the Twin Cam, the intake narrows to a diameter smaller than the valve seat bore, creating a bottleneck and turbulence, which is what you don't want in the intake or exhaust tracts. (Keep turbulence where it belongs, in the combustion chamber!) The simple

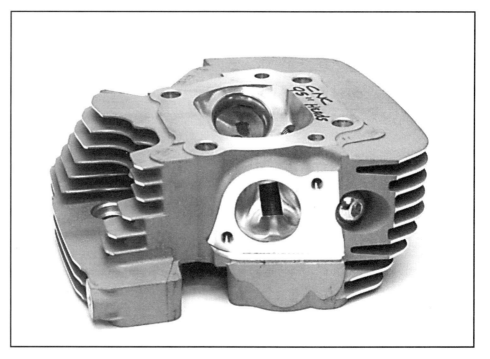

On the Twin Cam, the intake tract narrows until it gets smaller than the valve seat. The simple solution is to open up the port so that it blends with the valve seat, which is what was done on this Zipper's reworked head.

solution is to open up the port so that it blends with the valve seat. Once the intake tract is ported, the intake valve should get a fully-radiused valve seat, one that blends into the combustion chamber. Don't bother to polish the intake tract. Though it looks real impressive, it does nothing to improve the engine's performance.

As for the exhaust, installing a stock Evo exhaust valve, which is slightly bigger than the Twin Cam's (or a slightly larger one if the engine's specs require it), will do for the valve upgrade. The port, however, should be opened up to match the exhaust valve. The exhaust valve should then get a fully-radiused seat, just like the intake did so that it blends into the combustion chamber. And, as with the intake, don't bother to polish the exhaust tract.

As for the combustion chamber itself, the crew at Zipper's has found that the volume of the chamber can vary in size. To standardize the size of the chamber, Zipper's CNC-machines the chamber, as well as the intake and exhaust ports. This way, every head is ported and machined exactly the same, which means Zipper's can produce consistent performance numbers.

JET will rework your heads and then ship them back to you, ready to install. However, for the best results, JET suggests you run their manifold and specially-ground cams with its heads.

HEAD DOCTORS

So who can you go to when you're ready to get that engine breathing as it should with a set of better performing heads? There are three ways to go: You can send your heads out to be reworked, exchange your heads for a reworked set, or buy a new set of high performance heads. (Note: The following companies and most others that rework or exchange heads will not accept a head that has already been worked on.)

There are a number of companies around that will rework your heads. Donny Petersen of Heavy Duty Cycles in Toronto, Canada, has been reworking heads for decades and is well known for his performance work on Evo and Twin Cam engines.

Another TC head guru is Bob Johnson of Johnson Engine Technologies. I first met Bob when investigating a report that he was getting 100 horsepower and 100 ft-lbs. of torque from 80-cubic-inch Evo engines. I found that he can do that, as well as get great performance numbers for Twin Cam 88s. Bob, however, does not produce power using the conventional method of bigger ports and valves. He goes the other way and produces higher airflow velocities with smaller ports and valves.

The second way, exchanging heads, is how Zipper's Performance Products works. When you buy a set of Zipper's reworked heads, the price includes a core charge. Once you've install the Zipper's heads onto your engine, return your stock heads to Zipper's and they will refund the core charge. These heads have a fully-machined combustion chamber and CNC-ported intake and exhaust tracts, which flow 163 cfm @ 10" and 273 cfm @ 28". Zipper's states that its 95" kit can produce over 100 horsepower and over 108 ft-lbs. of torque when used with the proper exhaust and intake components.

If you're in the market for new heads, there are four companies presently supplying them for Twin Cam engines. Here they are, in alphabetical order, with their press release claims.

Edelbrock has two versions of its Performer RPM heads to choose from. The first has a 72cc combustion chamber, while the second has a 88cc one. For the best results, both heads should be used with Edelbrock's special JE pistons, which have domes that match the combustion chamber in its heads.

S&S Cycle offers its new Super Stock heads for Twin Cams, which have redesigned fins for increased cooling and rigidity and flow approximately 158 cfm @ 10" right out of the box. These heads come fully assembled and include all gaskets and hardware required for installation, as well as a special manifold. Two different combustion chambers (79cc and 89cc) are available to meet different displacement or compression requirements. These heads are available in natural aluminum or black powdercoat.

H-D's Screamin' Eagle heads use Screamin' Eagle valvetrain components and Evo cylinder head port shapes on its TC 88 SE heads, combined with the TC's bathtub combustion chamber. These heads offer a bolt-on compression ratio of 9.5:1 for an 88" (1450cc) engine and a 10:1 ratio on a 95" (1550cc) engine. However, when used with forged high compression pistons, both engine sizes will realize a 10.5:1 ratio. H-D recommends using a SE high tensile cylinder stud kit (P/N 16505-01) with its SE heads. (Note: Installing these heads, or any one else's, will void your warranty, even if an H-D mechanic installs them.)

STD offers heads, which are precision cast from 48,000-pound, tensile strength aluminum alloy, with STD's own high flow engineered ports and chambers. Various stages of finish are available including a hand blended valve job or full hand port and polish. Heads can be ordered bare or fully-assembled, with single or dual plugs, in vented or non-vented styles. Assembled heads come with 175-pound spring kit, retainers, seals, guides, and stainless steel valves.

CONCLUSION

It is our hope that, by this point, you have a better understanding of the good and bad features of Twin Cam 88 and 88B heads. As we stated earlier, if you are not looking to get substantial increases in power from your engine, the stock heads will do just fine. However, if you do want to get your engine's performance to increase dramatically, the stock heads must be either replaced or altered. They just will not flow enough air to allow the engine to develop its full power.

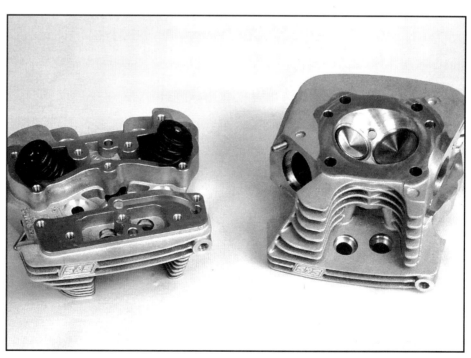

S&S heads come fully assembled and include all the gaskets and hardware required for installation, as well as a special manifold.

Hands-On

Three Assembly Sequences

BIG BORE KIT INSTALL

As we mentioned in Chapter Five, the way to get more power from your engine is to get more fuel/air mixture over the piston for the combustion event. And one of the methods commonly used to do that is increasing the size of the engine's displacement via increasing the engine's cylinder bores.

Once you have decided on this course of action, further decisions have to be made. For

Stock TC cylinders have plenty of "meat" and can be easily bored out and fitted with a set of aftermarket oversize pistons. Hackett

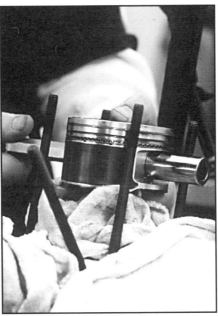

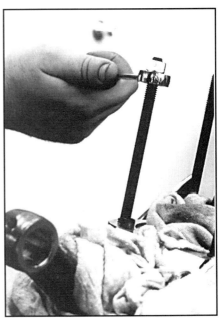

With the top end removed as per the H-D service manual, you can pull a wrist pin circlip out with a needlenose pliers.

Use a brass drift to push the wrist pin out of the piston. You may have to tap the drift with the palm of your hand to start it moving.

Remove the old cylinder studs and replace them with new H-D studs, which already have a thread locking compound on the threads.

starters, how big are you going to go? Though there are 95", 100", and 107" kits available, the most common is the 95 incher. Now, are you going to buy a big bore cylinder and piston kit from Screamin' Eagle? While this is an excellent kit, which consists of a set of Twin Cam cylinders with a 3-7/8" bore and pistons already fitted to the cylinders, it is expensive (this may be offset by other considerations, including warranty). All you really have to do is bore out the cylinders you already have, namely the ones presently on the engine, and have a set of pistons fitted to them. As we mentioned in Chapter Two, the Twin Cam's 3-3/4" bore cylinders have a very thick cylinder wall (almost 1/4"), which is thick enough to safely bore out to 3-7/8". In reality, that's all H-D has done with the cylinders you are buying with the Screamin' Eagle kit. Those are bored out 88" cylinders with Screamin' Eagle pistons filling the holes. H-D had a great idea with its 883 to 1200cc Sportster kits, which is exactly what they have done here. They made the stock cylinders walls thick enough to be bored out for an upgrade kit.

The installation that follows was done with a Wiseco kit. Wiseco offers big bore kits in two versions, flattop pistons with a 9:1 compression ratio,

or 10.5:1 domed pistons. These kits fit all 1999-2001 Twin Cam engines, both the 88 and 88B. If you send your cylinders to them, Wiseco will bore the cylinders out and fit the pistons to them for you, which is just what we did. Each 95" piston kit comes with two forged pistons, two complete ring sets, four circlips, two chrome wrist pins, and a top end gasket set, which is basically everything you need to do the job.

A great feature of the Wiseco pistons is that Wiseco's engineers have designed these to be a drop-in installation, eliminating the need to pull the lower end apart to re-balance. In addition, all Wiseco pistons for H-D are forged from the same alloy Wiseco specifies for use in its NASCAR and Indy-car pistons, for strength and dependability. These pistons also have anti-detonation grooves machined into the top ring land, which creates a turbulent flow of combustible gases that help seal the top ring to the cylinder wall reducing blow-by.

The accompanying photos show the bulk of what it takes to install a Wiseco 95" big bore kit with high compression pistons. There are also a number of important tips and facts that you should also know when doing this install, whether you use Wiseco pistons or some other brand.

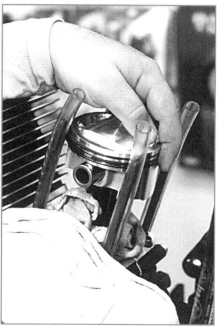

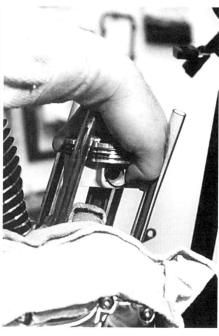

After you've checked the end gap on the compression rings, install the rings onto the pistons with a ring-expanding tool. Be sure gaps are staggered per the instructions. Don't forget the oil rings.

After you install one wrist pin circlip into its groove, slip the wrist pin part way into the piston. Then position the piston onto its connecting rod and send the pin the rest of the way.

You can now install the other wrist pin circlip into its groove in the piston. Then replace the cylinder base O-rings and oil drain dowel pin O-rings with new ones.

With a ring compressor and some oil on the piston and rings, slip the cylinder onto the piston. Gently work the cylinder down over the piston and onto the crankcases.

After cleaning the gasket surface with some acetone, place a new head gasket onto the cylinder.

Position the head on top of the cylinder and install the heads bolts, long ones on the right and short ones on the left. Torque the head bolts as per the sequence and values in the Manual.

58

The lower rocker box and gasket, goes on next. The long bolts with washers go on the left and the four shorts bolts with washers go in the middle and right. Leave them loose for now.

After you reinstall the push rod tubes fitted with new O-rings, slip the push rods into their tubes, black for exh. and silver for int. Then rotate engine so both lifters are at their lowest point.

The rocker arm assembly, complete with air/oil separator, can then go onto the lower rocker box. Torque all the bolts in the sequence shown in manual. Install top rocker gasket and cover.

INSTALLATION TIPS

• High compression pistons (greater than 10:1) require a high performance ignition module to match the ignition timing to the higher compression ratio, while the 9:1 pistons can be used with the stock ignition.

• These pistons can not be use with a stoker kit.

• Wiseco pistons are machined with valve pockets that are deeper and larger than the stock ones, which should provide adequate valve clearance for most performance cams. However, the valve-to-piston clearance should still be checked when installing high performance camshafts. (Ours had plenty of room, almost .140", but our valves had been set a little deeper into the heads to make room for a performance valve spring set.)

• The arrow on top of the pistons must always point towards the front of the engine when installed.

INSTALLATION TIPS

• The recommended end gap for the piston's two compression rings is .015". The oil rings require no adjustment. (See photo page 151.)

• After you use a needle-nose pliers to remove one of the wrist pin circlips, use a deburring tool to clean the circlip's groove so that the wrist pin comes out with minimal pressure. (That is, if you are not going to use the stock pistons in an engine again.)

• Don't reuse cylinder studs that have been torqued to spec. Always use new studs.

• Slip rubber hoses over the cylinder studs to protect the piston when you install it onto the connecting rods.

Hands-On: *Sequence #2*

HIGH PERFORMANCE CAMSHAFT INSTALL

As we stated in Chapter Five, the same companies that Evo owners have come to trust for their camshaft needs, such as Andrews, Crane, S&S Cycle, and Zipper's, to name a few, now offer excellent cams for Twin Cam 88s and 88Bs. Good thing, too, because cam selection is not something a novice should do. In fact, picking the right cams for your engine depends on a number of variables, like the owner's riding style, type of bike, and the components that are in, or will go in, the engine.

While we wouldn't go into an in-depth treatment of this subject here, we do want to point out a few facts that you should consider when choosing a camshaft for your Twin Cam. For starters, the best cam for a heavy touring bike will not be the best choice for a light Softail or Dyna. A heavy bike needs power down low, a torque cam, while a lighter bike can move the power band a bit higher, into the mid and upper ranges.

Also, unless you're aiming to hit the drag strip or win a horsepower shootout, don't pick a cam

Our starting point: The engine is open and ready to go. Everything has been cleaned and all the old cover gasket has been removed from the cover and engine. On a TC 88B, the tensioner screen should be cleaned, too.

that makes most of its power in the higher RPM ranges. Most people never even bring their engines up over 5500 RPM, never mind run their engines there often, so why buy a cam that makes most of its power where you don't plan on going? Besides, the more time an engine spends over 5500 RPM, the quicker the valvetrain components will wear out.

There are basically two types of cams available: bolt-in and those that require special valve spring kits. Bolt-in cams can be installed into an engine without having to do work on the heads, which we'll tell you about in a moment. However, just because a cam is considered a bolt-in, doesn't mean it won't require some clearance work in the gearcase cavity, though most do not. The best way to know is to check with the company you are buying the cam from. This way you're sure of just what is involved in installing that particular cam grind.

The hotter, or more aggressive, cam grinds will require the installation of a performance valve spring kit. These kits are a must because the stock springs will not have the spring pressure needed to operate the valves correctly with the new cam profile. Also, the valve springs will now be compressed more when the valve opens because of the new cam's higher lift, which means the stock spring's coils would hit each other (coil bind), or the top spring collar would hit the valve guide when the valve is fully opened. A performance spring kit matched to the cams will work with has these and other factors, which we won't go into here, taken into account. All that is needed is to follow the directions included with the kit and check the needed clearances during the install. (Note: Sometimes the valve spring openings in the lower box must be relieved a bit to clear the new spring pack.)

A common mistake of novices to the cam game is buying the hottest cam in the catalog just because it costs the same as one of the milder ones. To make use of that hotter cam, there has to be other performance work done to the engine. If you buy a radical cam with a high lift and long duration and shove it in a mild motor, you're not going to like the results. In fact, to quote a section from

We recommend installing new Torrington inside cam bearings using the proper tools. The stock bearings are fine for the stock cams.

Reinstall the oil pump with a new O-ring on its port to the right crankcase.

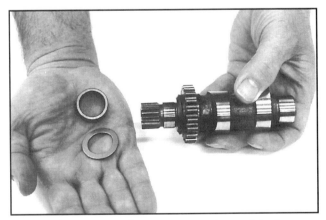

Press old cams out of cam support plate with the proper tool. Install new roller bearing's O-ring, thrust washer, and inner race onto the new rear cam as per manual.

Install new roller bearing for the rear cam and the ball bearing for the front one into the cam support plate. Install bearing retainer plate per the manual.

Note the pip mark on the tooth of each cam. Put a mark on the other side of the cam, on the same tooth, so you have them as reference marks later. Align the two marks as shown for proper timing.

With your marks aligned and the cams in the chain with the dark link oriented as before, press the cams (see the Installation Tips sidebar) into the support plate using the proper tool.

Use the proper tool to take the tension off the cam chain tensioner. Then pull the stay pin and swap it over to the outside of the support plate.

The cam support plate assembly can now be installed. Be sure to use Loctite 243 (blue) on threads. Torque mounting hardware for support plate and oil pump, which attaches to the support plate, to spec.

Before proceeding, make sure the two timing marks on the camshafts are aligned as shown. If they are, remove the secondary cam chain tensioner's stay pin.

the Andrews Products catalog concerning camshaft selection, "larger engines can take more cam than smaller ones. In other words, 88 cubic inches can handle a bigger cam than a 74 inch engine. More cubic inches can handle greater airflow from cams with higher lift or longer duration."

Actually, the best way to pick a cam is to first pick a company that you trust. Every major cam manufacturer has a tech department staffed with experts who will guide you through the cam selection process. Call them and let the pros know what you want the cam to do, what bike you are going to install it in, and what has been done, or will be done, to the engine, performance-wise. That way you end up with the best cam for what you have and need. If you are told that the amount of power you want will require more than just a new cam, it's time to start thinking about some of the topics discussed in previous chapters, namely other high performance work (Chapter 5), headwork (Chapter 6), and more cubic inches (Chapter 7).

That said, check out the accompanying photos to see how to install bolt-in cams into a TC 88 or 88B. Our bike for this install is the same 2001 Fat Boy equipped with a 88B counterbalanced engine that we put the big bore kit on in the last chapter. Whether your engine is a 88 or a 88B makes no difference, other than you should check and clean the screen for the balancer chain tensioners on an 88B.

INSTALLATION TIPS

• We recommend always using new inner and outer cam bearings when installing performance cams. We use Torrington.
• When installing new bearings, always press against the side of the bearing with the writing.
• The O-ring for the oil pump's port to the right crankcase is an upper push-rod O-ring. There are five of them in the H-D cam service kit that you should have for this install: four for the push rods and the fifth for the oil pump.
• If you are using a roller bearing in the cam support plate for the rear cam, which you should be, the rear cam can be wiggled into its bearing. You only have to press in the front cam.
• Though Twin Cam high performance valve spring kits are the same as an Evo's, their installed spring

height, which is a measurement that must be checked when installing a hi-po valve spring set, is usually too low. Seating the valves a little deeper into the head and taking some head material out below the lower spring collar will give you additional clearance.
• Some high performance spring sets may require some side clearance on the lower rocker box. Clearance to the top rocker should also be checked.

Note: All tools used in this sequence are from JIMS.

The two drive sprockets and drive chain, with the dark link facing as before, can now be installed. With the sprocket holding tool in place, torque the bolts to spec. Then remove tool and stay pin.

The cam (gearcase) cover can now be re-installed, followed by the lifters, pins and covers.

Section I - Chapter Seven

Hands-On: *Sequence #3*

INSTALL GEAR-DRIVE CAMS

Though we discussed several points worth considering when choosing high performance cams in the last chapter, we did not talk about the concern of some high performance engine builders regarding H-D's camshaft chain drive system. Some feel this system, which consists of two sprockets, two drive chains, two chain tensioners, and a chain guide, will not hold up under the loads placed upon it by a high performance valve spring kit for cam lifts of .560" or more. (The Motor Company offers Screamin' Eagle cams with lifts up to .569".)

S&S Cycles, which has been in the high performance game since 1958 and has set numerous speed records, decided to address this concern. What S&S did was take the simple and proven route; they went back to a gear-driven system. After all, the main reason why Harley-Davidson went to chains was

S&S gear-driven cams are offered in lifts ranging from .510 inch to .640 inch. These kits come complete with pre-lube and instructions. S&S

  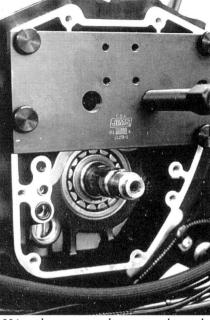

The start of the job: the cam cover is off and all of the old gasket is cleaned off. The gearcase cavity is clean and the oil pump is out.

Before proceeding, if you are working on a 88B, remove and clean the screen for the balancer chain tensioners. Reinstall it with a new O-ring.

Using the proper tools, remove the stock inner cam needle bearings and replace them with the new ones supplied in S&S' cam installation kit #33-5163.

because of federal noise regulations.

The only problem with a gear-driven camshaft setup, which was used in all previous overhead valve Big Twins in some form or another, was that it could not be made quiet enough for the feds, no matter how hard H-D tried with multiple cam and pinion gear sizes. The problem is that the fit between the teeth of the camshaft and pinion gears is loose when the engine is cold, resulting in a slight clattering sound in the gearcase. However, once the engine is at operating temperatures, the teeth mesh tightly together due to the steel gears expanding in the hot engine, which results in a whine. Neither of these conditions matter to the high performance builder, however, who is only concerned with better performance, reduced maintenance, and engine and part longevity.

Converting to the S&S gear-drive system has several benefits. Besides being a proved system, there are no maintenance issues with gears. No matter how well they are made, chains stretch and that means tensioners and guide shoes to keep them properly adjusted. These chains, and the components that service them, all wear in time and will eventually need replacement when used in stock engines. In a high performance application where

the loads imposed on the camshafts and therefore the chains and other parts, are much higher, these wear factors increase resulting in a shorter service interval.

Another benefit of gears over chains is less load on the cam bearings, which is why S&S recommends installing two ball bearings and not a rear roller bearing and front ball bearing as H-D now has to do to keep the rear cam bearing from failing. (See Chapter Four.) Without tensioners keeping the chains tight, the camshaft bearings only have to contend with the loads placed on them by the valve springs so ball bearings are fine. (Ball bearings are preferred because they spin with less friction than roller bearings, so more horsepower reaches the rear wheel.)

Then there's the fact that chain adjusting shoes and chain guides deposit debris into the engine's oil as these components wear. Gears do not need these components.

You can also use higher lift cam lobes with gear-driven cams because they rotate differently than chain-driven ones, resulting in more clearance between the lobes. (Cams with gears rotate in different directions, while chain-driven cams rotate in the same direction.)

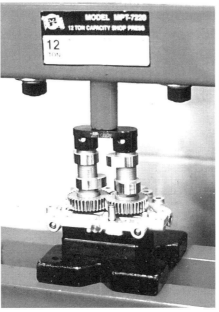

Reinstall the oil pump with a new pump-to-crankcase O-ring, which is the same as an upper push rod O-ring. Replace the O-ring on the face of the pump, too.

After you've reinstalled the bearing retainer plate and aligned the dots on the cams, press both new S&S cams into the cam support plate with the proper tool.

Here's how the camshaft/cam support plate assembly should look when you taken out of the press. The tool is on the ends of the two cams and the timing dots are aligned on the cam gears.

One more thing, the S&S gear-driven cams, which are offered in lifts ranging from .510" to .640" (the .510" is also available in a bolt-in, chain-driven version for mild engines), are much easier to install than the chain-driven variety. The accompanying photos will show you just what it takes to get these cams into your Twin Cam's gearcase, while the installation tips sidebar has some important additional information.

Install the cam support plate into the engine. Use Loctite 243 (blue) on all mounting screws and torque them to 95 in-lbs. as per the procedure in the H-D service manual.

Install the S&S pinion gear onto the shaft, with the timing dot on the tooth facing you. Use supplied pinion bolt and stock washer. Use Loctite 272 on the threads and torque to 25 ft-lbs.

The rear cam gear and key go on with the timing dot facing out and aligned with the pinion gear's dot. Install the S&S-supplied cam bolt (with Loctite 272) and washer, torque to 34 ft-lbs.

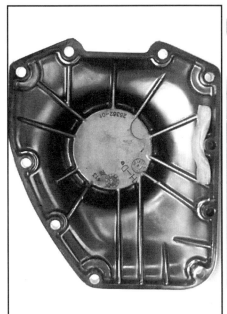

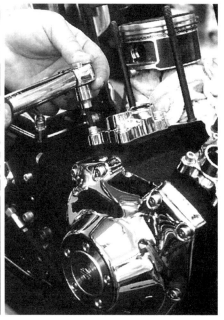

The clearance between the cover and rear cam gear must be checked per the instructions by putting some clay on the inside of the cam cover as shown.

You can then reinstall the cam cover, lifters and locating pins into their original locations. If you used clips to hold them in place, remove them now.

Install the lifter covers with new gaskets and torque the cover bolts to 95 in-lbs.

Installation Tips

• S&S' gear-driven camshafts are not compatible with the stock push rods. You must use S&S adjustable push rod kit #93-5095.

• We also recommend using S&S' camshaft installation kit #33-5163. This kit includes the new bearings and gaskets, but not oil pump O-rings, needed to install the camshafts and drive gears into the gearcase.

• You must have the H-D Service Manual on hand for the proper procedures, torque patterns, and torque specs to do this job right. Twin Cam engines, though they are superior, are not as forgiving as H-D's earlier engine designs. Twin Cams must be assembled as per H-D spec or engine damage will occur. You can bet on it.

• Though Twin Cams use the same high performance valve spring kits as an Evo, the installed spring height, which is a measurement that must be checked when installing the kit, is usually too low. Seating the valves a little deeper into the head and taking some head material out below the bottom spring collar will give you additional clearance.

• Some high performance spring sets may require side clearance on the lower rocker box. Clearance to the top rocker box should also be checked.

• If you are installing a 625G or 640G camshaft set, a small amount of material must be removed from the crankcase to allow .030" clearance for the inner camshaft lobes.

• Unlike chain-driven camshafts, both outer bearings are ball bearings on gear-driven cam installations, so the JIMS cam installation tool must be used on both cams.

• The new S&S rear cam gear is slightly larger than the stock rear sprocket. S&S calls for .030" clearance between the gear and the cam cover. Measure the clearance by putting some clay on the inside on the cam cover, as per S&S' instructions. Remove material if needed. (Our cover was fine.)

• Be sure to follow the procedure and torque pattern outlined in the H-D Service Manual for installing the cam support plate onto the crankcase and the oil pump onto the cam support plate.

Twin Cam EFI Systems

High Tech For The Old V-Twin

There are two types of sequential port fuel injection systems, also known as Electronic Fuel Injection systems (EFI), used by Harley-Davidson on their Twin Cam models. The first version uses the dual-throat Magneti-Marelli induction module. This system is found on Touring models, which use the rubber-mounted Twin Cam 88. The second version is the single-throat Delphi system, which is used on counter-balanced, solid-mounted, Twin Cam 88B Softails.

On the left, the dual-throat Magneti-Marelli one-piece induction module, which is used on Touring models. On the right, the single-throat, two-piece Delphi induction module is used on all counter-balanced, solid-mounted, Twin Cam 88B Softails. Note the MAP sensor on the Delphi unit.

Both of these systems work very well on stock bikes. Of the many EFI-equipped bikes we have test ridden, sometimes for thousands of miles, the throttle transitions from idle to various midpoint settings to wide open throttle is seamless. Once fired up, the engine runs smooth and throttle response is quick. With the exception of one Ultra back in 1999, we have never heard the engine ping or knock.

However, that's when the engine and the components that support it, like the exhaust system, camshafts etc., are stock. If you start making performance changes to the engine, even if you upgrade with Harley-Davidson's Screamin' Eagle Stage kits, many engines begin to run too lean, with owners complaining of poor performance, excessive engine heat, and pinging.

But before we get into why this is happening, let's first discuss what the main components of the two systems do, starting with the induction module, which is the part in an EFI-equipped bike that takes the place of a carburetor.

THE COMPONENTS

An induction module is the generic name given to the assembly that's responsible for taking in air and mixing it with fuel. This unit occupies the spot behind the air cleaner normally taken by the carburetor and intake manifold. The single throat, two-piece Delphi, which consists of a throttle body and intake manifold, is somewhat like a carb in that the intake manifold bolts to the heads and the throttle body bolts to the intake manifold. The dual-throat Magneti-Marelli unit also bolts to both cylinder heads just like an intake manifold on a carbureted bike, except this module is all one piece with no separate throttle body.

The induction module regulates the amount of air that enters the cylinders, much like a carburetor

does. However, instead of having a float bowl and metering jet system to deliver fuel into the incoming air stream, the induction module has two injectors that spray fuel into the intake tract. These injectors are mounted at the rear of the module, where it bolts to the cylinder heads. And although the pilot's throttle is connected to the throttle plate(s) of the induction module, the amount of fuel that gets delivered to the engine is controlled by a device called the Electronic Control Module (ECM).

The ECM is the brains of the fuel system. It is a solid state, sealed unit that is mounted under the bike's seat, or one of the side panels, depending on the bike. It's the ECM that opens the fuel injectors, which are electrically-operated solenoid switches, for the fraction of a second that's required to spray the right amount of fuel into the intake system. (The time an injector is open is called a *pulse width*.) The fuel supplied to the injectors comes from a fuel pump at a specific pressure.

The ECM is loaded with reference tables (like an old multiplication table, only much more intricate) called maps that tell it how long to open the injectors for a specific set of conditions. For example,

The two rectangular plug-ins at the rear of the module, are the fuel injectors. The two fittings next to them are for fuel supply (front) and fuel return (rear). The throttle position sensor (TP) is connected to the throttle shaft and mounts on the right side.

if the engine is at operating temperature, at sea level, on a 60 degree F day, with the throttle opened 25 percent, the ECM will reference the tables of data that are stored in its memory (by the H-D engineers) and find out what pulse width to use for this specific set of conditions. However, when the pilot opens the throttle more to go up a hill, or any of the other conditions change, so do the tables that the ECM references, which changes the injector's pulse width.

This self-adjusting sequence happens many times a second. In fact, the ECM is constantly readjusting the injector pulse width based on the information fed to it by a collection of electronic sensors located at various points around the engine and chassis.

THE SENSORS

The Magneti-Marelli system uses three primary sensors. These are the crank position sensor (CKP), throttle position sensor (TP), and camshaft position sensor (CMP). The secondary sensors, which are used to fine tune the system, are the engine temperature sensor (ET), intake air temperature sensor (IAT), and barometric pressure sensor (BARO).

The Delphi system, however, uses only the crank position sensor (CKP) and manifold absolute pressure sensor (MAP) as its primary sensors. The intake air temperature sensor (IAT), engine temperature sensor (ET), and throttle position sensor (TP) are secondary sensors, which help dial in the system, just as the secondary sensors do for the Magneti-Marelli unit. Let's take the sensors one at a time, starting with the Magneti-Marelli system's three primary sensors, then we'll cover the Delphi's.

The crank position (CKP) sensor is located on the front left side of the engine's crankcase. This sensor reads the 30 teeth that are cut into the engine's left flywheel. These teeth tell the ECM the engine's speed (RPM), while the two teeth that are missing establish the position of the flywheels in reference to Top Dead Center (TDC).

The throttle position sensor (TP) is mounted on the right side of the throttle body, so it can measure how much the pilot has opened the throttle plate(s).

The camshaft position sensor (CMP), which is not found on the Delphi system, is mounted inside the cam cover, under what used to be the ignition cavity cover. This sensor tells the ECM the engine's phase by sensing when the Hall Effect ridge, which is the raised section that goes halfway around the face of the rear camshaft sprocket, is passing by it.

As for the Delphi's two primary sensors, it uses the same crank position (CKP) sensor as the Magneti-Marelli unit. However, instead of using the throttle position sensor (TP) and the camshaft position sensor (CMP) for primary sensors, it relies on a manifold absolute pressure sensor (MAP). The MAP sensor, which is located on the top of the induction module, measures the pressure inside the intake manifold.

As for the Magneti-Marelli unit's secondary sensors, the engine temperature sensor (ET), which (you guessed it) measures engine temperature, is located in a well that's machined into the left rear section of the front head, near where the induction module attaches. The ECM uses the information supplied by the ET during the engine's warm-up phase to set the idle speed. Engine temp data is also used to determine the injector's pulse width at different throttle settings and conditions.

The intake air temperature sensor (IAT) is mounted on the left side of the throttle body. This unit measures the temperature of the air entering the intake system. The ECM uses this info to determine air density.

The barometric pressure sensor (BARO) is mounted right in front of the ECM unit. This sensor allows the ECM to compensate for altitude changes by monitoring atmospheric pressure. By the way, the data access port, which is what the mechanic plugs the analyzer into when testing the system, is also located right in front of the ECM.

The Delphi system also uses an engine temperature sensor (ET) and intake air temperature sensor (IAT) as secondary sensors. However, the throttle position sensor (TP), which the Magneti-Marelli system uses as a primary sensor, is a secondary input on the Delphi.

Though there are more parts to the system, like a fuel pump, etc., these are the components that directly affect the way the engine performs from second-to-second. And, as we said earlier, these two systems work wonderfully, as long as everything remains stock. Once you start making changes, however, you run the risk of ruining, not helping, your engine's performance.

The reason for this dilemma is locked up inside the ECM. As stated earlier, this sealed unit tells the fuel injectors how much fuel to spray into the air passing through the intake tract based on what tables the H-D engineers put into its memory. Too much fuel, and the engine will run too rich. Too little fuel, and the bike runs too lean, which is the problem many owners are experiencing once performance changes are made to their bike. The tables in the ECM's memory, which can not be changed or adjusted, are too lean once changes are made. Even owners that have installed the component packages specified by H-D, including the ECM changes and injector changes, have found that their engines are running too lean. Also, installing performance parts on an EFI-equipped bike that would normally be great upgrades on a carbureted one, can make the engine so lean it will not run at all.

POWER COMMANDER II

Enter Dynojet's Power Commander II. This device plugs into the stock wiring harness of a Magneti-Marelli EFI-equipped bike (only) and allows the mechanic to adjust the signals sent out by the ECM to the fuel injectors. It does this by recalculating the signals from the EFI system's sensors. This tricks the bike's stock ECM into thinking it needs more fuel that it would normally allow for the existing conditions, which enriches the air/fuel mixture enough to operate an engine with performance parts installed. The folks at Dynojet call this sensor offset technology.

The PC II comes with a CD containing several fuel maps, which can be downloaded via a Pentium personal computer using the supplied cable. (Note: The PC II must be mounted on the bike with the ignition on to download anything into it.) Included with the PC II is a software package, which allows you to fully map the fuel and ignition curves on your PC and then download them into the Commander. You can also ask the techs at Dynojet to load the map you need into the PC II unit before they send it to you. This fuel curve can then be fine tuned, whether it's one of your own or one of Dynojet's, using the three touch buttons on the unit's faceplate. We've installed this unit in a number of bikes and have been able to resolve many owners' performance complaints using the maps on the PC II's CD.

As good as this sounds, the PC II can alter the signals coming from the sensors only so far. Engines with a 95-inch displacement and extensive headwork can not get enough fuel to run right. In fact, larger

engines will not run at all. Engines of 95" and some minor performance work is the limit to what the PC II can handle using the stock injectors and ECM chip. However, Mike Daniels at Dynojet states that if the stock fuel calibration cartridge (chip) is swapped out for the one supplied with a Screamin' Eagle Stage II kit, and a set of higher flowing injectors from Frank Bao of the Eagle Motor Company is used instead of the stock units, you will not have to "lie" as much to the ECM with the PC II to get the fuel you need sprayed into the intake system, which may solve the problem for the bigger displacement engines. By the way, you can alter the engine's ignition curves as needed with the PC II, too. You Softail owners were not forgotten. The Power Commander IIIr, which was introduced in November 2000, is the unit you'll need to dial in the Delphi system on your bikes. This Power version Commander uses direct injector control technology, which means the PC IIIr alters the signal that comes out of the stock ECM, not from the sensor's to the ECM. That means large displacements and extensive headwork are not a problem with the PC IIIr. And, just like with the PC II, you can alter the engine ignition curves as needed, too.

If you are contemplating making some major performance modifications to your EFI-equipped bike, we suggest you call the techs at Dynojet first and check that what you want to do is not outside of the limits of the Power Commander you must use.

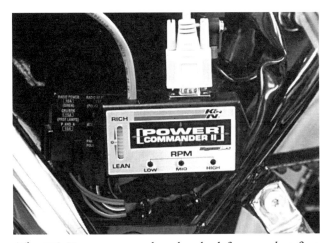

The PC II gets mounted under the left cover, but first we downloaded a new map with a Pentium laptop computer via the Dynojet-supplied cable.

Tool Time

Almost Like the Snap-on Truck

The only thing most of us lust after more than motorcycles is tools. So what could be better than a bunch of tools designed specifically for fixing motorcycles - TC models in particular.

Most of what you see here are specialized tools needed for engine work and most of those come from JIMS. We've even included a new scanning tool for V-Twin riders ready to enter the new milenium.

Two tools from JIMS: On top, a connecting rod bushing tool (#1051) used to remove and replace a wrist pin bushing without removing the connecting rod from the crankcases. The other is a cam chain tensioner tool set (#1283) used to unload the pressure on the primary and secondary chain tensioners. JIMS

Similar to the Evo cam bearing tool, removes inner bearing easily and without damage. Won't let rollers fall down inside the case. JIMS

This Zipper's cam relief tool allows the TC 88 engine builder who is installing any cam grind other than stock to do a smooth, professional job of machining two relief channels into the crankcase. The tool bolts to the crankcase and uses the inner cam bearings to support the cutter spindle. Features adjustments for cutter diameters and thread depth feed.

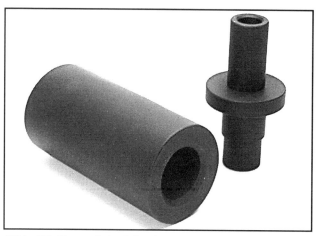

This JIMS crankshaft bushing tool, which is piloted for accurate operation, will remove and install the crankshaft bushing in the support plate.

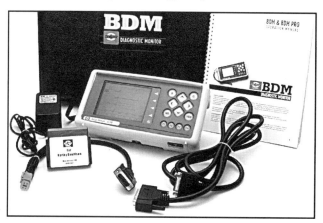

JIMS offers a new diagnostic scantool by BDM for TCs. The H-D specific software included with the tool allows the user to retrieve trouble codes and display sensor level outputs in an easy-to-read format.

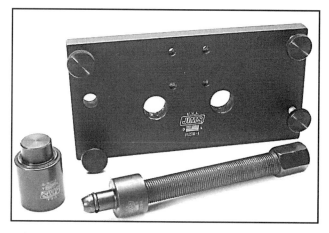

This JIMS inner cam bearing installer tool will install the two inner cam needle bearings. It perfectly aligns to the shaft bores for a precision press fit.

How Fast Do You Want To Go

Think First

Like building a new bike from scratch, or deciding on a complete paint job for your Dresser, the most important part of modifying the engine is the part that happens before you take the tools out of the tool box.

Planning, that boring step that most of us would rather skip, is just as important as the installation of the camshaft or the new ignition. Because the cam you choose, and whether or not it works with the rest of the components in the engine, is what will

The bags on this Perewitz-built Road King say Dresser, yet the custom paint and abundant billet say bar-hopper. Knowing which will be the bike's primary use helps in designing and building the appropriate engine.

Are you looking to do some serious drag racing late on Saturday night or at the local strip? Or are you the more typical rider simply looking for more passing power and a better rush when you twist the throttle up against the stop.

Tuners and aftermarket shops complain that many Softail models don't come with tachometers, so those riders don't really know how many RPMs the engines are turning on the highway or where they typically shift. "They think they're turning

Bob Belanger's scratch built bike is built for speed rather than comfort and uses a 98 inch S&S engine with HSR 42 carburetor from Mikuni. Note the Ness covers, Perewitz boxes and missing lower fins.

ultimately determine how well the engine runs and how fast it is or isn't. The more power you want, the more important the planning becomes.

What makes this job of building a great engine so tough is not only the fact that we're talking about your favorite two-wheeled conveyance. We're also talking about picking just a few key components from among literally thousands that are offered for sale. It isn't that some of the parts are "bad." Most of the carburetors, pipes and ignition systems offered for sale in this market are high quality items. The issue is whether or not they are the best items for the job at hand. Will they work (in combination with the other parts already on the engine) to provide you with more power while retaining good rideability and dependability.

HOW WILL THE BIKE BE USED?

If you ask nearly any engine builder how they pick the right components for a particular engine being built or modified, they all say the same thing: "The owner needs to tell me how the bike will be used and ridden." It's not enough to say, "I want more power." You need to define how much more power you expect, and where in the RPM range you want that power.

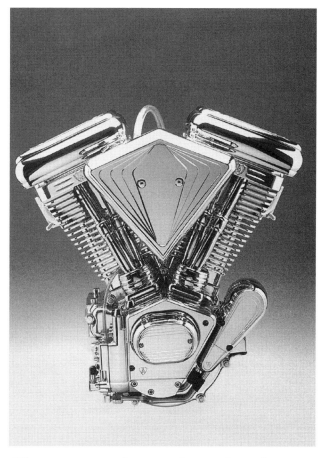

There are more and more options to choose from these days, including complete engines up to 120 cubic inches like this billet-beauty from Cory and Arlen Ness.

really high RPMs," says one tuner, "but they really don't know, and it makes it hard to know what to sell them." Legendary drag racer and engine builder Nigel Patrick says he tries to build engines "that have really good response between 1500 and 3500 RPM because that's where most of us ride most of the time." Yes, most of us do most of our riding at low and mid RPM, and would do well to avoid cams and combinations of parts that don't come on until the engine is turning four or five thousand RPM.

In the interview with Doug from Head Quarters, the bike's end-use *and* weight become issues in planning out the engine modifications. Doug is only comfortable putting high compression engines in light bikes. Like a number of experienced V-Twin mechanics, Doug likes to match the camshaft with the compression ratio, which brings up the whole issue of combinations, a topic that comes up again and again in this book.

YOUR OPTIONS

When it comes to more power you can either stay with the stock 80 inch displacement, increase that displacement, or throw in the towel and pop

for a complete new big-bore engine.

The "hot rod 80" is the easiest way to get more power from your stock or near-stock Evo-style engine. The term hot rod 80 is pretty loose and includes everything from a motor with aftermarket pipes, a new air cleaner and a rejetted carb; to a true hot rod engine with a high lift cam, aftermarket heads, aftermarket pistons and a S&S carburetor. Chapter Five takes a long look at this concept and the various combinations of parts that can be used to make good, usable horsepower and torque.

Increasing the displacement of your engine is a sure way to add power. You can increase either the bore, the stroke, or both. In either case you will be forced to split the cases, either to install new flywheels, or to have the cases bored out to accept new cylinders with larger diameter spigots (the area at the base of the cylinder that fits down inside the cases). At this level you're probably spending more money on parts, labor or both, than in assembling a hot rod 80. You will find more on exactly what it takes to create a 89 or 97 cubic inch Evo in Chapter Five.

If you're building a bike from scratch, or nothing but the best will do, then you probably want to step up and buy a complete aftermarket engine. The most popular units from S&S, TP Engineering, Merch and others offer 107, 113 or 120 cubic inches. These engines can be purchased complete, ready to install, or in pieces, so you or the engine builder of your choice can carefully check the balance of the wheels and the internal clearances. Purchasing the engine disassembled allows you to paint and/or polish all or part of the engine (though many of the engines are now available already polished). Chapter Six takes a look at the big-block options, including a shop tour at TP Engineering.

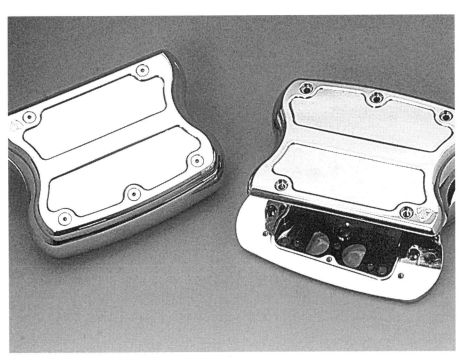

Many covers and accessories are offered in either polished or plated finish. Not only is the chrome brighter, it stays that way with only a minimum of maintenance. Arlen Ness

MAKING SENSE OF IT ALL

Deciding among the many options means deciding what it is you really want. If it's just a

Paint with Powder

Designing an engine means designing the finish on the outside, as well as the parts on the inside. At Arlen's shop they offer customers a full menu of options, including powder coating done in-house.

POWDER COATING 101

Most powder coating paint starts as a dry polyester powder. Finishes range from flat black to high gloss available in a wide range of colors, including candies and clearcoats. Powder isn't sprayed in the conventional sense. It's an electrostatic charge that causes the powder to attach itself to the part being painted.

Air pressure is used to move the powder from a large hopper to the gun, where the powder particles pick up a high negative charge. The barrels or heads have a positive charge relative to the powder, and it's this difference in voltage that creates the attraction between powder and part.

POWDER AT ARLEN'S

When Jon Nelson "sprays" a set of barrels the paint drifts up in a cloud or mist, moving in slow motion toward the parts being coated. Despite the electrostatic attraction between paint and part, it still takes a careful painter to ensure the powder is drawn into all the recesses between the fins.

As with any painting operation, John tapes off areas where he doesn't want any paint, like bolt holes or cylinder bores. Instead of 3M masking tape however, these parts are masked off with some very special high-temperature polyester tape. Areas like the fins, which were polished earlier, can simply be wiped off after the powder is applied and before the parts go in the oven.

The bake cycle in the small oven is what makes the powder bond to the part so tenaciously. Because of the heat, used parts must be fully disassembled and really clean, so the heat won't ruin any seals or drive oil from the pores of the metal. Jon also reports that some aftermarket barrels measured before and after coating did change shape slightly, so it's best to coat first and machine second.

And though the powder is available in nearly any color, it's generally easier to match the liquid paint to the powder, than the reverse.

Jon coats the barrel with a spray gun that looks more like a timing light. The output of the gun is controlled by the control box at his left.

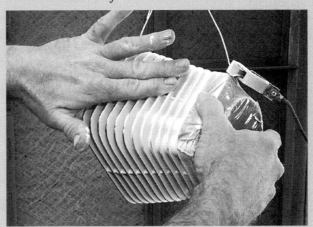

After spraying the powder, it's an easy task to carefully wipe the powder off the polished edges of the fins. Note the tape on the base of the barrel.

Baking at roughly 375 or 400 degrees is what turns the powder into shiny "paint" and causes it to bond to the object that's just been painted.

little more power, the answers are easy and readily available. If it's a lot more power, or enough to pull a ten-bottom plow across a field, there are still plenty of good options though you're better check the balance in the checkbook before ordering parts.

Once you know what you want take the time to decide what it will cost. If you're doing most of the labor yourself, you only need to determine the cost of the parts. Be sure to leave room for those outside

This project bike from Andrews uses a limited edition 110 inch S&S engine with (yes, an Andrews cam) a S&S "G" carb, hidden under a Perewitz air cleaner.

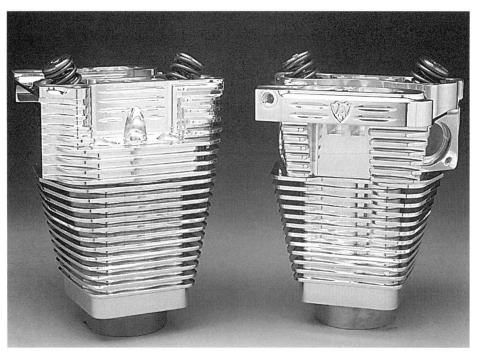

Billet is more than just a buzz work in the aftermarket industry. Because billet parts are cut, they have a more precise look with sharp edges. And because the billet is so hard, they also polish to a very high shine. Arlen Ness

services that can't be done at home, things like porting, machining and cylinder boring.

Sometimes it's good to work through two or three scenarios. More money will often (not always) get you more power. That doesn't mean that twice the money will get you twice the power. Check out the interview and combinations discussed in Chapter Five. Talk to some good local shops and experienced mechanics. Look at web sites for companies like Zipper's and Headquarters and S&S and a dozen more. Check their available packages and their cost. Don't just look at peak power, study the dyno charts to see the kind of horsepower and torque curves that result from the various modifications.

You wouldn't build a house without looking at various plans and working through a budget. Likewise, it's not a good idea to build or modify an engine without considering different ideas, products and combinations of parts.

INTERVIEW: DON TIMA

Don Tima is the engine builder for Donnie Smith Custom Cycles. To say that Don is a perfectionist is an understatement. His attitude toward cleanliness can be described with a story: Don's friend Jeff needed his Harley worked on. Knowing Don, Jeff made it a point to wash the bike before bringing it to the shop. Somehow the bike still wasn't really "clean" however, and the first thing Don did was take the bike to the self-serve car wash.

Don, how long have you been wrenching on Harleys?

Since 1978, since I was in high school. Eventually I got a job at a dealership, Belmont Harley-Davidson in St. Paul. They sent me to Milwaukee to the invitation-only factory service school.

Don, give us a combination of parts that works good on the street, a fairly mild 80 inch engine?

Well, I'd use a Crane 2862B fireball camshaft and the factory CV carb with a Head Quarters jet kit and no change to the spring or slide. I would mill the heads to create some additional compression. For pipes I would use the Vance and Hines Pro Pipe or a decent collector pipe, a 2 into 1. For a more traditional look the Python pipes work pretty well. The Harley header pipes with the cross-over pipe make good horsepower. Drag pipes are my least favorite, straight pipes are non-horsepower pipes. They only work wide open and there's always a transition point where they stutter.

What if you could build a wilder engine and weren't limited to 80 cubic inches, what would your combination be?

I like a short stroke with a big bore, so I would go with a 3-5/8 inch bore and stock flywheels. For heads I would start with a pair of factory heads from 1984-1986, those are good castings, then I would do some port work. I would use a Head Quarters cam, the Thunder Plus or Lightning, depending on what compression ratio I had. (I would want at least 10.5 to 1). I'd use the S&S lifter limiters, so they don't squeeze out at over 5000 rpm. I would degree the breather gear to get rid of that wind. For a carb you could still run the CV, but I might change to a S&S Shorty G. Same exhaust as before, the Thunder Header is another one that makes good power.

If I were going to go still further I'd add roller rockers, the S&S Shorty G or QuickSilver carburetor and nitrous. Nitrous is cheap power, but it can be hard to set up and tune.

What about some of the mistakes that people make building street engines?
Too many mis-matched components, they buy stuff that's not designed to work together. And they buy a carb but they never dial it in. The way the carb is delivered the bike will start and run,

but it's far from right. The manufacturer can't make one carb that works with 400 applications. They're either lean, which means the bike runs hot and scores the cylinder; or they're rich and the extra gas washes the oil off the cylinders which scores the pistons.

Riders need to ask around, to find a good shop they can trust, or at least parts that work together. And they have to be careful of the exotic stuff. The S&S Hot Set Up kits are a good example. They come with the right cam, and jetting instructions for the carburetor.

Over-caming and over-carbing are the two biggest mistakes people make. They get a cam for a 96 inch motor and put it in an 80, thinking it's the hot ticket, but it's not.

Can a fairly mechanical person do his or her own top end installation?
Anyone with a little mechanical aptitude and some literacy can put in new pistons and a camshaft. You have to be able to read and you have to get a service manual. Then you have to READ THE MANUAL, don't read it after you've screwed it up. The key is to read it first.

What do pulleys have to do with engines? Nothing, except that they determine the RPM at any given speed and are thus an important part of the performance equation. CCI

Section II - Chapter Two

Carburetors

The Mixing Bowl

Note: Much of this chapter applies to TC as well as Evo-style V-Twins.

WHAT IS A CARBURETOR

A good carburetor is one that will supply a regulated quantity of air and fuel to the engine under all operating conditions. This means that no matter how hot or cold the engine is or how quickly you whack open the throttle, the engine will receive the correct amount of fuel for optimum operation. A tall order indeed.

One of the all-time best selling aftermarket carburetors, the S&S Super E and G have a huge following. A butterfly design, proponents of the "Shorty" carburetors like the fact that the carbs are easy to set up, and tuck in nicely on the right side. S&S

At the heart of nearly any carburetor is a venturi, or a restriction of some kind in the carburetor throat. As Mr. Bernoulli discovered more than 200 years ago, when you force air through a restriction in a pipe the speed of the air increases as it moves through the restriction. As the velocity goes up the pressure goes down. Think of the fast moving air as being "stretched" so it has less pressure. Now if we introduce gasoline at this low pressure point in the venturi, subject to atmospheric pressure at the other end, the gas will be "pushed" out into the air stream where it can atomize and mix with the air on its way to the cylinders.

The simple carburetor described above might work on a constant speed engine, one that never changed speed. In the real world we need a means of controlling the flow of air through the carburetor and some additional fuel circuits. A good carburetor is designed to work in three "conditions," often described as: idle, low speed and high speed. Most carburetors have these three basic circuits, and more, with air-bleeds and other provisions to ease the transition from one circuit to another. A few carburetors are "seamless" examples that possess only one tapered needle that moves farther and farther out of the main jet in response to

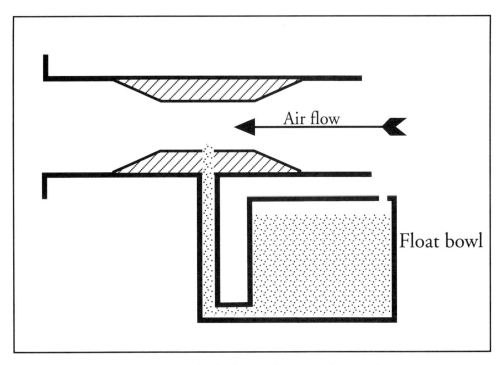

At the heart of every carburetor is a venturi, a restriction in the pipe. Air pressure within the venturi is reduced, so gas (under atmospheric pressure) flows to the venturi where is is atomized and mixed with air.

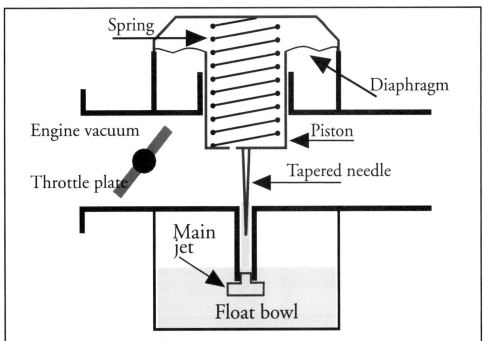

A CV carburetor uses a floating piston to create a variable venturi the size of which is determined by engine speed and load. Higher speeds create increased vacuum which works against the spring to open the venturi. As the piston moves up the tapered needle is pulled farther out of the orifice - providing more fuel.

Q&A: Bob Yost

Bob, let's start by giving us some background on you and how you got involved in this business?

Well, it really started when I put an aftermarket carb on my bike and it ran pretty bad. So I started looking at the carb and figured there had to be something that could be done to make it run better. The key of course was atomizing the fuel and I started looking for a way to do exactly that. I felt the performance could be increased by increasing atomization.

So tell us what a Power Tube is and how it works?

It is an emulsion tube. It breaks the fuel up into smaller particles. Instead of a single stage emulsion tube, you now have a two-stage emulsion tube. You're doing a better job of atomizing the fuel. Smaller particles are easier to move and distribute. It takes less vacuum to move the smaller particles so you get better throttle response. You get better combustion and better performance. Better heat transfer too.

You could use the analogy of wheat. With a stock carburetor the fuel coming out the main discharge tube is like wheat – big heavy particles. With our Power Tube the fuel coming out the main discharge tube is more like flour. The flour moves and mixes with the air in the carburetor throat much more easily than the wheat. It also burns more readily.

Your power tube kit comes with various main jets and two needles. Can you give me a series of steps buyers should follow in determining which jet and which needle to install to match their particular engine?

Essentially, the deal is, if you run it a little rich it's just a little rich and a little sluggish, that's OK with me. Then you can make it leaner in stages. Too lean is worse, it creates additional heat and can damage your engine. Eighty percent of the callers have what you might call a stage one bike. It's a mild hop up job. For them it's a matter of swapping jets. I suggest they go one or two sizes larger than stock on the main jet. If it's a 175, then put in a 185. Note: This is for a CV carb. Going from a 175 to a 185 is considered two steps. Also, CV jets are metric, measured in millimeters. A 175 is 1.75mm. and a 185, is 1.85 mm. The S&S carbs use jets measured in inches, so a 72 has a hole .072 inches in diameter. But before they swap any jets they should get a service manual and read it. The manual is an invaluable source of information.

Sometimes they have a problem I can diagnose over the phone. Did it spit or pop as you accelerated through an intersection? That's needle position. Did it spit or pop at cruising speed? That is too small a slow speed, or pilot, jet.

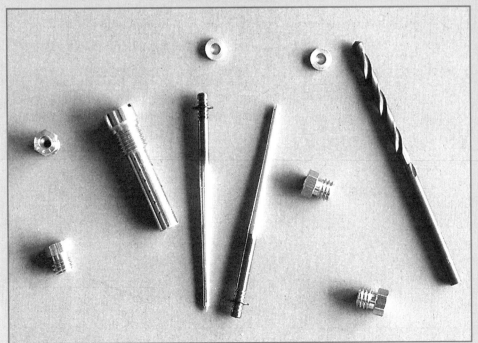

The Power Tube kit for a CV carb comes with two needles - adjustable for position - the Yost emulsion tube, a drill bit (for accessing the idle-adjustment screw) and a series of main jets.

Next, when you're running at 65 mph in fifth and it rattles or pings when you nail it, your main jet is too lean. Oil temperature is another good indicator. The oil temperature should be 190 to 210 at the oil bag. Over that and you're in trouble, something is wrong.

What are the mistakes that people make?

Sometimes they add a wild cam, and then drag pipes. That combination is great on the track but terrible on the street. I tell them to get a Bagger-type cam and free-flowing mufflers or a good two-into-one exhaust system.

What about the CV piston spring and the size of the hole in the CV piston?

I say, do not cut the spring or run a lighter spring, it's a recipe for disaster. The slide opens too quick and you loose vacuum in the carburetor throat and that slows down acceleration. In terms of the hole in the CV piston, I don't like to see them open the hole any bigger than 1/8 inch, and I prefer a hole smaller than that on a heavier bike. With Bagger-type bikes, or bikes with straight pipes, a 7/64 inch or .109 inch, hole is about right.

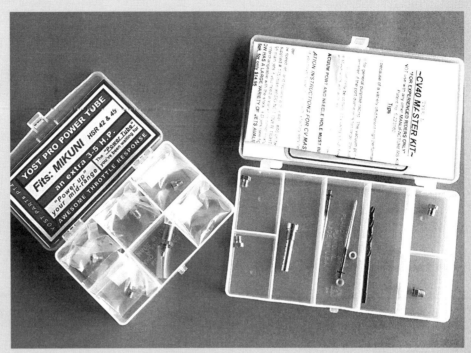

The Yost kits area available for Mikuni and Keihin CV (shown) as well as most models of the S&S. Jet kits are also available.

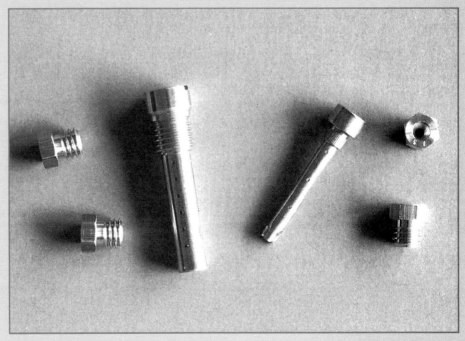

Most carburetors use an emulsion tube to mix some air with the gas before it hits the venturi. The Yost power tube (CV style on the left and S&S on the right) is simply a more efficient emulsion tube.

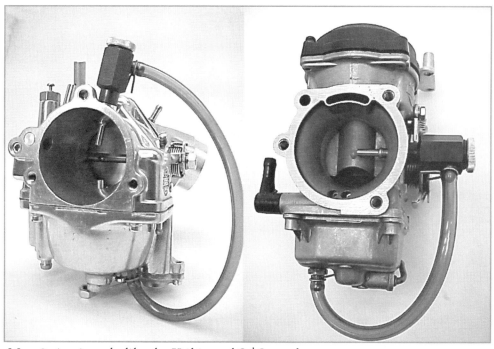

Most 2 circuit carbs like the Keihin and S&S use the high-speed circuit from 2500 to 6000 rpm, a very wide range. The Thunderjet can be installed and used as a 3rd circuit, over 4500 rpm, allowing the high-speed circuit to be tuned for good midrange. Zipper's

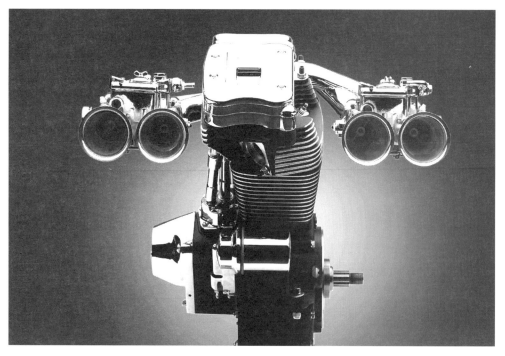

Weber dual throat carburetors are suddenly very popular and available in sexy twin-carb setups like this one. Each carb, available in 40, 45, and 48mm sizes, feeds one cylinder. CCI

either throttle position or engine vacuum.

Even with a provision for controlling the airflow at various speeds, real-world carburetors have to deal with situations like cold starts and sudden acceleration. A cold engine needs an extra-rich mixture for example, because gas doesn't like to atomize with cold air. Sudden acceleration, on the other hand, means the amount of air passing down the throat of the carburetor increases instantly, while the heavier fuel takes considerably longer to catch up.

So we add a choke or enrichment circuit for cold starts and an accelerator pump, though some carbs don't need one, to squirt a little extra gas down the carb throat when the guy in the SUV suddenly comes up along side and tries to cut you off.

When trying to describe carburetors it seems there are as many exceptions as there are rules. So rather than continue describing a theoretical carburetor it might be easier to jump right in with descriptions of the various types of carburetors and follow that up with a brief look at each of the most popular carburetors currently on the market.

CARBURETOR TYPES
Butterfly Carburetors

A fixed venturi carburetor, also known as a butterfly carburetor, has a fixed restriction in the throat. A "butterfly" valve is used to control the amount of air flowing through the carburetor throat. Fuel for high speed operation is usually introduced at the venturi while fuel for idle and low-speed operation is often introduced into the throat closer to the butterfly valve.

Less complex, and less expensive, single Weber setups are also available. As with any carburetor, the most important thing is whether or not it clears your right leg. CCI

Supporters of this design cite the fact that butterfly carburetors have been used on everything from Model A Fords to Harley-Davidson motorcycles. In the aftermarket, the S&S carbs are the best-known examples of the butterfly design.

Constant Velocity & Slide Carburetors

Some carburetors vary the size of the venturi in the carburetor throat according to throttle position or engine load. These variable-venturi designs come in two basic models (more later). Usually the slide or variable restriction is connected to a tapered needle that passes through the main jet. In this way increases in venturi size are tied directly to increases in fuel.

There are two styles of variable-venturi carburetor: the constant velocity design, which we often call a CV carburetor, and the straight variable-ven-

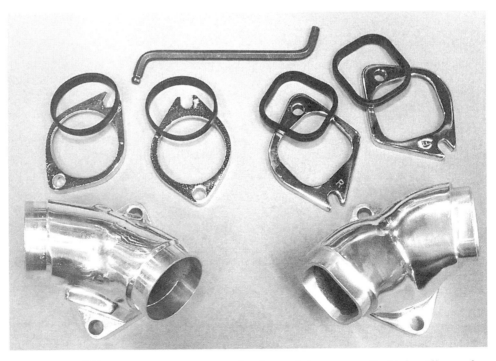

Intake manifolds come in a vast range of styles and sizes - one of which will match your engine, (including the design of the ports) and carburetor.

turi design, often called a slide carburetor.

In the constant-velocity design the throttle is connected to a conventional butterfly valve. Upstream from the butterfly valve is the variable restriction in the carburetor throat. This restriction is held in the closed position by a spring and opens according to vacuum within the carb throat. More vacuum causes the piston to open farther, increasing the size of the venturi. At idle for example, both the butterfly and the venturi are closed. As the throttle is opened more vacuum is applied to the slide piston, the piston moves up until equilibrium is achieved between the spring pushing down and the vacuum pulling up.

As the slide or piston moves up the tapered needle is pulled out of an orifice, effectively increasing the amount of fuel. The most common

CV carburetors in the aftermarket are the Keihin carb used on factory bikes since the mid-1980s (now available in a larger size through SE) the seldom seen SU, and the billet carburetor from Carl's. Adherents of the CV carburetor design point out the fact that these carbs only open up to admit as much air as the engine can use under a particular load. You may open the throttle, but the piston will only open as far as needed. This keeps air speed through the carburetor nearly constant (thus the name) and aids throttle response.

The non-CV carbs with variable venturi are usually known as slide carburetors. These designs eliminate the butterfly altogether and connect the throttle cable to the slide. The slide is connected to a tapered needle that passes through the main jet. As you open the throttle the slide opens the ven-

For the ultimate in the Chopper look, try a downdraft Weber on this stand-up manifold, available with velocity stacks or air cleaner. Remember that if the carb is higher than the bottom of the gas tank you will need a fuel pump to push the gas uphill. CCI

turi allowing more air through the carburetor throat. At the same time the tapered needle is raised in the jet, effectively increasing the size of the jet and adding more fuel to the increased air flow. The most popular slide type carburetors include the Mikuni and the QwikSilver II.

Fans of the slide or smooth-bore designs like the fact that by eliminating the butterfly you eliminate a major obstruction in the carburetor throat and create the "smooth bore," a bore that will pass more air (with less turbulence) for a given size than any other design.

If you like the CV design but need something bigger than the standard 40mm design, Screamin eagle now offers a 44mm CV carb and manifolds for Evo (shown) or TC.

THE RIGHT ONE FOR YOU

Whether your V-Twin is a mild 80 cubic inch street motor or a 120 inch brute with a four-inch bore, there's a carburetor out there that's right for you, actually three or four carburetors. Once again the trick here is not to pick a "good" carburetor, but rather the one that's right for your application.

In choosing a carburetor for your engine you need to consider how it fits the bike, will it interfere with your right leg (extra critical if you're running forward controls) and what style air cleaners will fit the carb. A few of the bigger

Designed by Patrick Racing, this chrome plated manifold mounts two 42mm slide carburetors. Available to fit most Evo-style V-Twins, kit comes with velocity stacks or billet air cleaner. Arlen Ness

The Mikuni PAT kit (Pass A Truck) is another good example of components that are chosen to work together as a package - each assisting the other to improve performance. CCI

carbs may not clear the five gallon Fat Bob tanks. Be sure when you buy the carb that you get the right style and length of throttle cables. If you want your carburetor in show chrome, note that some of the current aftermarket carburetors are available in polished or chrome plated versions, while other manufacturers insist you *not* chrome plate their carburetors. Check with the manufacturer regarding the availability of extra shiny renditions of your favorite carburetor.

The single most important thing to consider before buying the carburetor is how it will work in relation to your particular engine. If you have a good shop doing all or most of the work on your engine consider their suggestions before buying a new carburetor. Ask around to be sure the carb you want is easy to tune and that jets and other parts are readily available. Remember bigger isn't always better and sometimes a carburetor that's too big results in low air velocity in the carburetor throat and poor low-speed response. This last comment is particularly true when considering some of the smooth-bore designs.

Because the emphasis of this book is street engines, some competition-type carburetors have been left out of the following product descriptions.

Rivera knows that people want their carburetors hangin' out there for all to see, and have designed this tilt-forward manifold to accept S&S E and G carbs when mounted on most factory engines as well as many models from S&S. Arlen Ness

WHAT'S OUT THERE
The Keihin CV carb

The most common CV carburetor out there today is the Keihin, used for years and years by Harley-Davidsons on both their Big Twins and Sportsters. Though a lot of people poo-poo the "stock" factory carburetor, there is nothing wrong with using a Keihin on a modified engine. New emulsion tubes, slide kits and jets of every size imaginable are available to help this carb meet the demands of most modified V-twin engines. For anyone working on a budget, or modifying a Milwaukee-built bike, the use of a Keihin makes all the sense in the world.

The Keihin supplied on factory Evo engines uses a 40mm throat, big enough for most modified Evos. According to Doug at Head Quarters the 40mm CV is big enough for everything up to (and possibly exceeding) 95 cubic inches. For those who like the idea of a CV and find the stock Keihin too small, Screamin' Eagle now offers a 44mm CV that looks like a 40mm Keihin, just bigger.

QwikSilver II from Edelbrock

From one of the largest automotive aftermarket parts suppliers comes the QwikSilver II carburetor. The QwikSilver II is a flat slide, variable-venturi carburetor available in sizes ranging from 36 to 42mm. All sizes are available in two mounting styles, flange mount or grommet mount.

Some interesting innovations exclusive to the QwikSilver include a single fuel circuit controlled by a single needle that is the same width from top to bottom with a tapered flat section cut out of the back side of the needle. As the air passes through the venturi past the needle it creates a low pressure area which allows the fuel to move up the pickup tube and into the venturi where it atomizes instantly as it hits the airstream. As the throttle is opened farther by the rider the needle moves out of the pick-up tube allowing more fuel to flow past the needle.

Another feature of the QwikSilver is the ability to self-compensate for altitude changes. The float bowl is vented to the venturi rather than the atmosphere like most carburetors. By venting to the venturi the float bowl is pressurized with the same pressure as air traveling through the venturi.

New to the QwikSilver line is their "pumper" series carbs. While the original carbs did not have an accelerator pump, the QwikSilver is now available with or without an accelerator pump and in enough sizes to adapt to nearly any V-Twin. For anyone who needs visual as well as mechanical bang, the QwikSilver can be ordered in a dual-carb setup with polished manifold that puts the two carbs way out there on the bike's right side. Any questions regarding the QwikSilver should be directed to the QwikSilver division of Edelbrock (see Sources).

Introduction to the Keihin CV carburetor. Take four screws out of the top of the carb and the CV piston, spring and diaphragm emerge. Needle is seen hangin' on the bottom of the slide.

89

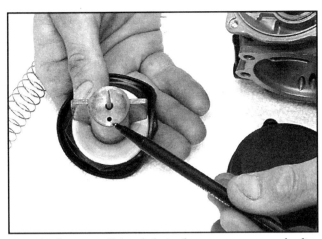

On the bottom of the slide is the vacuum port, the little hole that causes so much controversy over whether or not it should be enlarged.

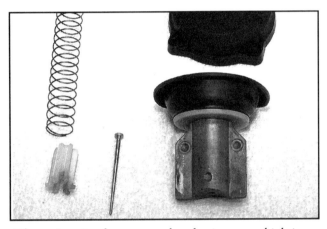

The spring sits down onto the plastic seat, which in turn holds the needle (which is non-adjustable in this case) into the piston. The seat must hold the needle tight in the slide.

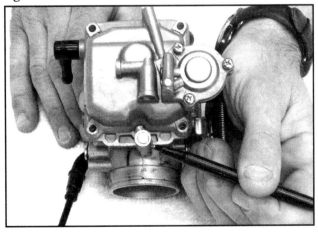

On the bottom of the carb is the plug that covers the idle screw. For adjustment, "three turns out is a good place to start" says Don Tima.

Super E and G from S&S

The Super E and G carburetors from S&S are among the most popular of the many carburetors available for Big Twins. These two "shorty" carburetors are both butterfly designs measuring 1-7/8 inch (47.6mm) for the E, and 2-1/16 inch (52.3mm) for the G, measured at the throat. These two carburetors are designed to tuck neatly into the right side of the bike.

Features of the Super E and G include an easy-to-reach idle mixture screw and changeable mid and high-speed jets. Instead of a choke an enrichment circuit is used. This "choke" lever is located in a convenient position at the back edge of the air cleaner.

With two sizes available the S&S Shorty carbs will work on everything from relatively small displacement V-Twins to strokers and big-bore engines. The S&S Shorty carburetors are designed for dual cable operation. S&S also makes a 2-1/4 inch Super D for monster motors and race bikes.

Screamin' Eagle carburetors from Harley-Davidson

Milwaukee now offers no less than four Screamin' Eagle carburetors, either as stand-alone items or as part of their extensive selection of hop up kits.

For fans of butterfly carburetors, SE offers a 40mm butterfly style carburetor designed for high airflow and increased horsepower throughout the RPM range. This carburetor from The Motor Company features an accelerator pump and three fully adjustable circuits. The Screamin' Eagle carburetor is designed to operate with a two-cable throttle system and comes with a high-flow air cleaner. Also offered in the SE catalog is a 42mm flatslide carburetor manufactured by Mikuni. Designed to work with stock cables and SE air cleaner and breather kits this carburetor is said to offer "exceptional throttle response and driveability."

Looking rather automotive is the newest offering from SE, the Holley/SE two barrel carburetor. This carb is part of a complete induction system, including an open-plenum manifold, designed from the ground up for late model Harley-

Davidsons. The Holley carb uses stock cables and comes in either as-cast or polished versions.

Mikuni

Long known as the manufacturer of high-performance fuel-mixers, Mikuni has recently added more models to its line of slide-type carburetors. The new 42mm and 45mm carburetors are intended to answer the carburetion needs of large displacement V-Twins. The 45mm in particular is intended for all-out performance applications only. All three Mikuni carbs, they offer a 40, 42 and 45mm, feature a roller bearing slide assembly for precise movement and a light return spring. The new larger carburetors come with a larger capacity fuel bowl and an adjustable accelerator pump.

Like other carburetors of this type the Mikuni "smooth bores" have no butterfly in the throttle bore to restrict air flow at full throttle. This means that a 40mm Mikuni, the recommendation for mild 80 cubic inch motors, will often flow more air than a larger carb of a different style.

A final note: All the manufacturers I talked to in assembling this section stressed the importance of properly matching the carburetor to the particular engine it will be used on. Be sure to read all the manufacturers recommendations and call them before buying if you have any doubts. Try to buy your carburetor from a reputable local shop, one that can help with tuning tips or parts you might need for the installation.

Buying from a good shop will minimize the tuning you need to do after the installation. Though many of these are shipped with the jetting set close enough that the bike will start and run, there's a good chance that the bike will be either too rich or too lean, meaning possible damage to the engine. Ask the shop that's supplying the carb for their recommendations. If you do decide to swap a jet, be sure to think first. People often change the wrong jet, like changing the high speed jet to cure a mid-range problem controlled by the low speed jet. This is when it's nice to have access to good advice from the local shop, or on the other end of the manufacturer's 800 number.

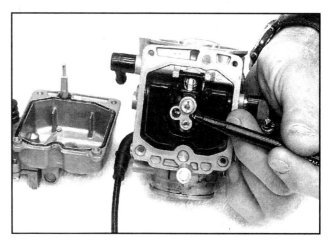

The pen points to the main jet, located on the bottom of the emulsion tube.

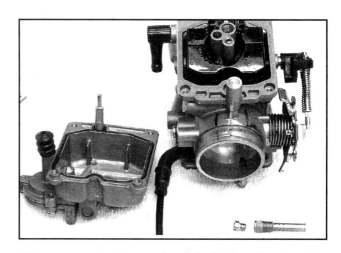

Here you see the inverted carb body, float bowl and the main jet, which screws into the main jet holder, or emulsion tube.

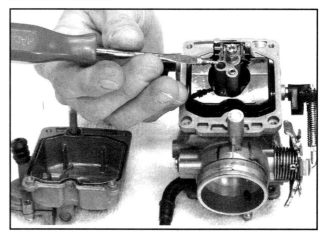

Here is the "other" jet, the slow or pilot jet, just unscrewed from the recess in the carburetor body.

Camshafts

More May Not Be Better

CAMSHAFT BASICS

Before trying to discuss how to chose the right camshaft for a given V-Twin it might be helpful to discuss the basics of camshaft operation and the terms used to describe each camshaft.

First, let's consider each of the four strokes and how the camshaft affects, and is affected by, the power, exhaust, intake and compression strokes. Because the camshaft runs at half the speed of the crank the camshaft will turn one complete revolu-

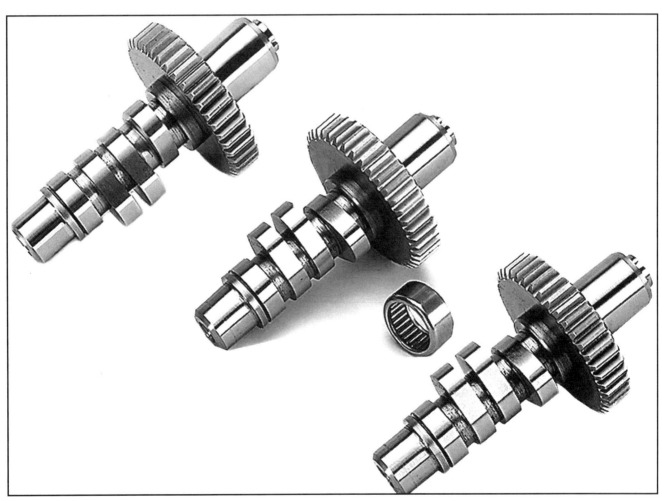

Camshafts come in every lift and duration imaginable. The trick is to find the right one for your bike - one that works with the compression ratio and goals for the engine.

tion to the crankshaft's two. Remember too that most cam specifications are given in degrees of *crankshaft* rotation. Finally, the cam in a Evo-style V-Twin runs backwards from engine rotation, which confuses people.

POWER STROKE.

On the beginning of the power stroke, with the piston approaching TDC, both valves are closed. A spark causes pressure in the cylinder to build, forcing the piston down in the cylinder. As the piston nears the bottom of the cylinder the pressure, and power production, drop off. In order to get as much of the spent gas out of the cylinder as possible the exhaust valve opens before the piston actually reaches BDC. With a typical mild street camshaft the exhaust valve opens at about 60 (crankshaft degrees) before the piston hits BDC.

EXHAUST STROKE

The exhaust valve is open as this stroke begins, and stays open during the entire 180 degrees of the exhaust stroke. In order to pack as much fresh gas as possible into the cylinder, especially during higher RPMs, the intake valve opens before the piston hits TDC. This period when both valves are open is known as the overlap period, during this time the outgoing exhaust gasses help to draw the intake charge in behind them. Typical street cams begin opening the intake valve at about 30 degrees before the piston reaches TDC during the exhaust stroke.

Crane makes cams with a removable gear that allows the timing to be advanced or retarded from stock - as well as conventional cams with pressed on gears. Crane

The Andrews EVO27 is a bolt-in cam that works great in heavier Dresser-type bikes, especially when combined with a mild compression increase, better exhaust and a re-jetted carb. Andrews

INTAKE STROKE

As the intake stroke begins both valves are open. By about 25 degrees past TDC the exhaust valve has closed, ending the overlap period. The intake valve remains open during the rest of the intake stroke.

A 104 degree intake lobe centerline means the crankshaft will have turned 104 degrees when the intake lobe is at maximum lift.

COMPRESSION STROKE

Though it would seem best to close the intake valve when the piston hits BDC, the gas and air are coming into the cylinder with a certain momentum (especially at higher RPMs) and the piston doesn't really start to build pressure until it has traveled part way up into the cylinder. For these reasons the intake valve stays open into the early part of the compression stroke. A typical street cam closes the intake valve at about 40 degrees after BDC.

CAMSHAFT TERMS
VALVE LIFT

Lift is simply the amount the valve is lifted off the valve seat. The specifications are for net lift at the valve, as it is affected by the ratio of the rocker arm (V-Twin ratios for Evo and TC-style engines are 1.625 to 1). More lift would seem to add more power, though there are trade-offs here just like everywhere else. For example, open the intake valve too far, too quick, and it runs into the piston. Even if it doesn't run into the piston, the higher the lift (at a given duration) the faster it must move in going from the closed to the open position. Moving the valve too fast puts enormous stress on the valve train and requires stout springs, which creates even more stress. If the lobe gets too extreme the effect on the valve train is like hitting the parts with a hammer.

Valve lift is also limited by the spring. A given spring can only be compressed so far before the coils bind. As discussed elsewhere in this book, the valve lift and cam profile must be matched to the valve springs so as to avoid coil bind and keep the lifter following the camshaft even at high RPM. Most camshaft manufacturers will provide recommendations for spring pressure, and when a particular spring kit should be installed. Note: With very high lifts the spring collar may hit the rocker cover.

DURATION

Camshaft duration is simply the amount of time the cam holds the valve open, measured in degrees of crankshaft rotation. When comparing duration figures from one cam to another, it is important to use the correct duration specification. In order to keep everything equal most manufacturer's give a duration specification *after the lifter has achieved .053 inches of lift.* Use this specification to compare camshafts, not the advertised duration, which is usually considerably larger. More duration would seem to be a good thing for power production, except that by lengthening the duration you effectively shorten the compression stroke. Which is why you need a good match between the engine's static compression ratio and the duration.

As a rule of thumb a cam with longer duration will have more power higher in the RPM range than a cam with less duration. A camshaft with less duration will tend to have better power on the bottom end and a better idle quality. Too much duration on the street will give you a bike with no

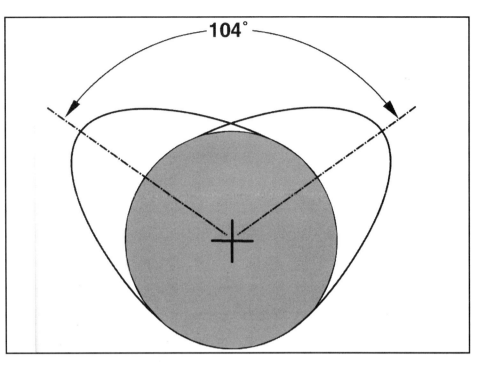

Lobe separation angle is simply the distance in degrees between the centerline of the intake and exhaust lobes. A narrow separation angle will provide more valve overlap.

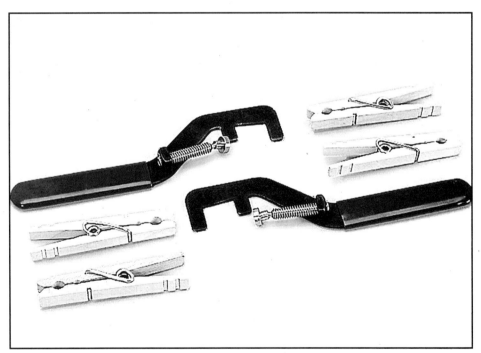

This tool kit from Crane makes cam installation in an Evo much easier. Crane

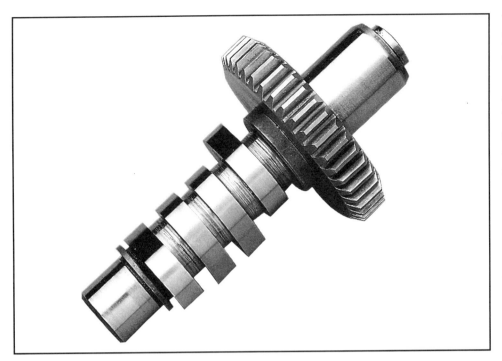

The RevTech 10 is designed to produce power from 2000 to 6000 RPM in light bikes like FXRs, Dynas and Softails. Works best when used with aftermarket exhaust and re-jetted carburetor. CCI

From RevTech comes this adjustable breather valve designed to allow the engine builder to change the timing of the breather to match the engine's displacement. Made from steel, they come with 4 different thrust washers for correct fit. CCI

bottom end - no power at lower RPM where you tend to need it most.

Overlap, as already described, is that period of time when both the intake and exhaust valves are open. As time goes on fewer and fewer manufacturers provide a specification for valve overlap.

Lobe Separation Angle

This is the newer specification that is often provided instead of overlap. It is the distance in *cam degrees* between the centerline of the intake and exhaust lobe. A 104 degree lobe separation angle means the centerline of the intake lobe is separated from the centerline of the exhaust lobe by 104 degrees. Similar to overlap, the separation angle is more comprehensive. Not only does it include overlap information (a narrow angle means more overlap) it provides more valve timing information than the simple overlap specification alone. In general, a cam with more overlap and a smaller separation angle will tend to have a power band that is "peakier" and occurs at a higher RPM than a cam with less overlap and a larger lobe separation angle.

Intake lobe centerline.

This is a timing specification and gives the position of the piston when the intake valve is at its maximum opening. If the intake lobe centerline is 104 degrees the crankshaft will have turned 104 degrees past TDC at the point when the intake valve has maximum lift.

Measured in crankshaft degrees, intake lobe center-line can be compared with the lobe separation angle to indicate the amount of advance the camshaft has relative to the crankshaft.

Fully understanding how intake lobe centerline affects engine performance requires a short explanation. At TDC, or 0 crankshaft degrees, the cam has both lobes pointed up, this is the middle (or roughly the middle) of the overlap period and also places the cam in the approximate middle of the lobe separation angle. If the same cam with an intake lobe centerline of 104 degrees had a lobe separation angle of 104 degrees it would be said to be 0 degrees advanced.

In other words, starting at TDC, the piston moves down through 104 degrees of crankshaft rotation, or 52 degrees of cam rotation to put the intake valve at maximum lift. Because 52 is half of the lobe separation angle, the cam was in the middle of the overlap period (half the lobe separation angle) when the piston was at TDC. If the same cam with the lobe separation angle of 104 degrees had an intake lobe centerline of 100 degrees, then the cam is said to be 4 degrees advanced - this cam would reach maximum intake lift after 100 degrees of crankshaft rotation, or four degrees sooner.

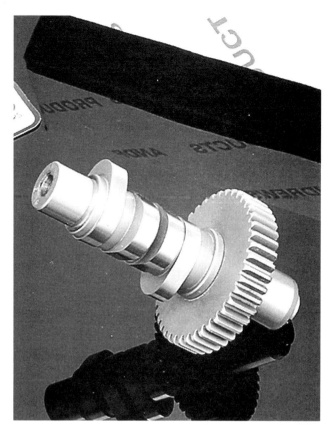

Andrews makes everything from mild bolt-in cams to high lift race-only grinds. All are cut from bearing-quality steel on computer controlled machines.

Lift at TDC

This is simply the net valve lift when the piston is at TDC. The information can be plugged into a formula (more later) that can be used to determine whether or not there is sufficient valve to valve clearance to prevent a collision between the intake and exhaust valves. While valve-to-valve clearance can be determined from a formula, there is no mathematical means of determining valve-to-piston clearance. When installing radical cams, most engine builders mock-up the

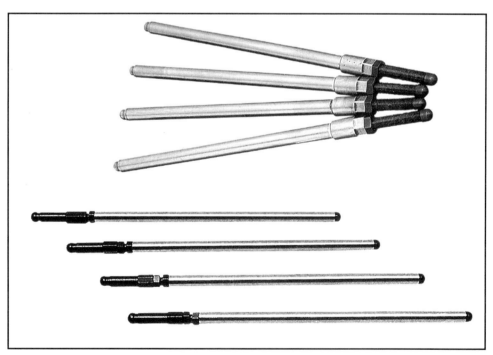

Nearly any cam change will require the use of adjustable pushrods. On top, a set of time-saver pushrods from Crane (see chapter 02/07). On the bottom, a set of conventional adjustable pushrods from Andrews, available in aluminum or chrome-moly.

engine with clay on the valve cutouts in the pistons. After rotating the engine, they disassemble and then measure the clearance between valve and piston. Note: These clearance and valve spring issues are discussed in more detail in the Cylinder Heads chapter.

PUTTING IT ALL TOGETHER

Designing a cam is very much a matter of matching the lobe shapes, lift, duration and timing to a particular set of operating conditions. Timing is always crit-

Most aftermarket cam gears are sized someplace in the middle of the size range. Gear fitment can be checked with the cam cover in place and no spacers on the cam. To quote John Andrews: "If you're sliding the cam in and out of the engine (reaching in through the lifter block hole) and you can feel a slight drag between the gears, that's probably a pretty good fit. You can also reach in and rotate the cam forward and backward. If you can feel backlash with your fingertips it's too much. Ideally the backlash should be zero. If the engine whines after it's started the gears are too tight. That can cause damage. If the fit it too loose it can get into some rattling. It's annoying but it won't hurt anything. It usually occurs only at low speeds."

Cam and pinion gears can be measured with pins of a specific diameter, as shown here on a Sportster gear. Most mechanics however, work by feel. Andrews

ical on a V-Twin cam to ensure that the two valves don't run into each other, or the piston. The Andrews catalog lists their cams as either "stock," meaning they can be used with stock valve springs, or "high lift," meaning they require the use of springs with additional pressure, and a check of installed height and clearances when the heads are assembled.

As mentioned again and again, there needs to be a good match between the cam duration and static compression. Though you can ruin a street engine with too much duration, you can also use a little "too much" duration in a motor with high static compression pressure to bleed off some compression pressure at low speed - and thus allow the engine to run a higher compression ratio than might otherwise be possible.

The cam that's right for your bike will depend on a whole list of variables, including the carb and pipes, the compression ratio, the shape of the ports, valve size, the bike's weight and the type of riding you do. Getting that perfect cam means asking the right questions and being honest about the type of power you want and your riding habits.

WHICH CAMSHAFT IS RIGHT FOR YOU

The Crane Cams Motorcycle catalog has a long list of things you should consider when choosing a camshaft for your particular bike. The comments (which echo those of other builders interviewed in the book) list the important criteria as: riding style, weight of bike, operating range, engine displacement and compression ratio, and engine modifications and accessories.

They go on to explain that when it comes to camshafts, "the 'bigger is better' belief... is usually far from the truth." and that, "The camshaft provides an 'RPM power band' that is approximately 3000 RPM wide. This RPM power band can be produce in either the lower range (idle to 3500 RPM), in the mid range (2000 to 5000) or in the high range (3500 to 6500)."

The engineers at Crane advise that achieving a particular performance goal means you must produce the right amount of power at the correct RPM range. If your bike is heavy they advise using a cam with less duration as an aid to get that weight moving.

Compression pressure is often affected by the camshaft choice. In particular, cams with more duration result in decreased cylinder pressure, in which case you would want to offset the loss by designing an engine with a higher compression ratio. The catalog explains that, "This is why the descriptions of the camshafts may note that an increase of compression ratio is recommended with a particular design."

Before closing the section on camshaft choice, the catalog explains that bigger engines (more cubic inches) work better with camshafts that have increased duration and lift. Their final piece of advice should perhaps be set in bold-face type. "It is important to put correct component parts on the engine that will work together and enhance the desired performance."

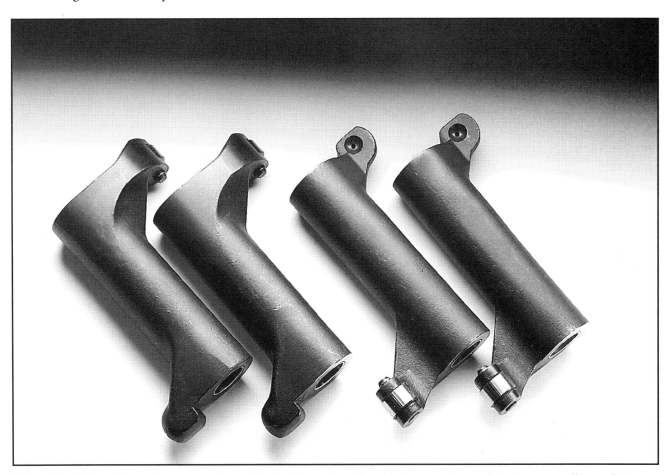

These RevTech roller rocker arms reduce side loads on the valve during opening and closing, as well as reducing friction. CCI

Section II - Chapter Four

Heads and Porting

Managing Airflow

There are a wealth of new cylinder heads, both cast and billet, on the market today. The emphasis in this chapter, however, is on the set up and porting of factory heads. And though this chapter is in the center of the Evo half of the book, some of the porting information regards the newer, TC heads.

BEFORE YOU BOLT THE HEADS ON

Note, some of this material is borrowed from an earlier Wolfgang book: Ultimate V-Twin Engine.

Whether you plan to assemble the heads your-

Some heads, like these Evo castings from S&S designed for 3-1/2 or 3-5/8 inch bore, have a combustion chamber shape that dictates a specific piston-dome shape. S&S explains that these are "high quench combustion chambers designed to promote turbulence - the good kind - and enhance flame travel."

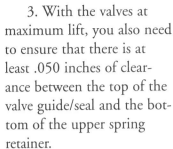

3. With the valves at maximum lift, you also need to ensure that there is at least .050 inches of clearance between the top of the valve guide/seal and the bottom of the upper spring retainer.

4. Though you need clearance before coil bind, you also need a spring with enough pressure to keep the lifter rollers following the cam lobes at high RPM. Some builders like to use a set of springs matched to the camshaft, but even then you need to check for coil

Setting up a head at Zipper's starts after the valve job and porting are done. Before the real assembly begins there are a number of things to check.

self, or pay someone else to do the work, it's a good idea to know what kind of clearance and valve spring pressure issues can arise. Spring pressure and clearance problems become more critical with wilder, high lift cams. What follows is a list of concerns, most of which can be ignored when installing mild, or "bolt in" camshafts.

1. Possible valve to valve clearance problems. To quote Lee Wickstrom from Lee's Speed Shop, "As you get into wilder cams and heads with bigger and bigger valves, you need to pay more attention to this matter." You can either check the clearance physically while the head is in a fixture like that used with the flow bench, or you can use a formula, like that provided by Andrews.

2. Possible valve spring coil bind. You need to know the dimension of the spring when it "stacks." Most cam and valve-gear manufacturers recommend that you have .050 to .060 inches of extra clearance between maximum lift and coil bind. It's obvious that you shouldn't lift the valve to the point where the spring hits coil bind. Less obvious is the fact that if your cam/head/spring combination has the spring *near* its coil-bind limit at each camshaft rotation the springs will soon fatigue.

After assembling the head with light springs, the installed height can be checked.

bind and clearance to the top of the valve seal.

5. Valve to piston clearance. Though it sounds like too much extra work, professional builders recommend assembling the engine with clay on the valve pockets of the pistons, rotating the engine by hand a few times and then disassembling to make sure the clay is at least .080 inches thick where the valve came closest to the piston. This is one more reason why it's so much easier to work with a known combination of parts.

The spacers seen here can be added under the spring base to increase pressure, but the spring will coil-bind earlier as a result.

The installed measurement is now transferred to the "real" springs installed in the Baisley machine - which gives a reading for seat pressure at that height.

SHOP TOUR: SET UP A HEAD AT ZIPPER'S

This work is done at Zipper's Performance Dan Fitzmaurice, owner of Zipper's, starts the head assembly with a bare head. At this point the valve job and porting work are already done.

Before starting on the assembly, Dan provides a brief discussion of valve springs. "The valve springs must be a good match for the cam. In Zipper's opinion, lots of Harley-Davidson engines are assembled without enough spring pressure. Too much spring pressure is not necessarily as hard on the valve train as people might think. There needs to be a balance here because out-of-control valves are harder on the valve train than high spring pressure. Get a spring pressure recommendation from the camshaft manufacturer or from the local cylinder head expert."

Dan starts by assembling the head with a light spring installed in place of the real valve springs. Now he can measure the installed height. With a Baisley machine he can install the valve spring he wants to use at the specific installed height and check the spring pressure.

If the pressure is too light a shim can be placed under the spring, but you can only add so many

Checking For Valve To Valve Interference

If your heads have larger valves or new seats installed or if a new performance cam has been installed, being able to easily check for possible valve to valve interference will be helpful. For all H/D heads it is possible to do a simple calculation to see if valve to valve interference might be a problem which will need attention.

1. Andrews Products lists valve lifts at TDC (Top Dead Center) on all cam instruction sheets. Write down the number for your cam. For an EVO59 cam, the TDC lift = .233 inches (see data on page 7 of the catalog).
2. Minimum valve to valve clearance should be .060 inches.
3. Calculate the minimum valve separation distance as follows:
minimum Valve Separation Distance = TDC lift + clearance.
4. For EVO59 cams, Minimum Valve Sep. Dist. = .233 + .060 = .293.
5. Measure the minimum separation between the two valves **when they are seated** (as in diagram). If actual measurement is not at least .293 inches, modification will be necessary to avoid valve to valve interference.

(Cut seats deeper or back cut valves).
6. Remember, this technique is NOT for piston to valve clearance.

Borrowed with permission from the Andrews Products catalog.

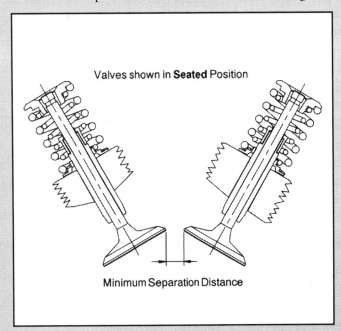

Valves shown in **Seated** Position

Minimum Separation Distance

shims before you reduce the amount of travel available to the spring before it "coil binds." In some cases you might have to use a different spring to achieve the correct pressure and travel at a given dimension.

To check for coil bind, Dan compresses the outer spring, with upper and lower collars (and any spacers) in place and records that dimension. (Warning: A compressed spring is kind of like a time bomb. Be sure it doesn't detonate - get loose - while you have it compressed.)

Because he knows the installed height, Dan can make sure that the total valve lift plus a clearance factor won't compress the spring to the point of binding. The Andrews Camshaft people feel you should have .060 inch as "clearance" before spring bind occurs. Minimum spring height should equal the stacked height plus the .060 inch clearance plus the maximum lift of the camshaft.

Note: it's a good idea to check installed pressure and clearance before coil bind even with springs

that were shipped as part of a kit - because the manufacturer of the spring has no idea which set of heads you own or exactly how the valve seat is positioned in the head (all of which is affected by any porting work and valve jobs that have been performed on the head).

Dan explains that you also need to be sure that the upper spring collar doesn't contact the top of the valve guide or seal at total lift. To check this he compresses the valve the full amount (with the light spring in place) and checks the clearance between the bottom of the upper spring retainer and the top of the guide and seal.

With regard to possible valve-to-valve clearance (which should be checked before the valve job) follow the Andrews procedures outlined at the top of this page.

PORTING A HEAD
Shop Tour, Lee's Speed Shop
More than one good mechanic has drawn the parallel between engines and air pumps, with the com-

ment: "the more air you get in and out the more power you make."

Getting more air into the engine, and more exhaust gasses out, means more than just bolting on huge carburetors and the latest trick exhaust. Whether you're talking Evo or Twin Cam, some of the biggest restrictions to good air flow are found in the heads themselves. To get a better idea what's involved in a good porting job we spent an afternoon at Lee's Speed Shop (formerly Fritz T. Wilson Racing) in Shakopee, Minnesota.

THE FIRST STEP, THE VALVE JOB

A good porting job, whether it's an Evo or Twin Cam, starts with a good valve job. Lee wants the actual seat (the area where the valve seals against the "seat") to be as close to the outer edge of the valve as possible, because this in effect makes for a larger diameter valve and port (some heads get physically bigger valves, which we will get to in a minute). Lee

moves the sealing surface closer to the edge of the valve in a series of cuts:

1. First a 45 degree stone is used to eliminate the current sealing area.

2. Then a 30 degree cutting tool is used to take some material off the upper part of the seat and define the upper edge of sealing area.

3. Next comes a 60 degree cutting tool which Lee uses to define the lower edge and the width of the sealing area. Note: For street use Lee likes to see a sealing area .040 inches wide for the intake and .060 for the exhaust seat. The wider exhaust seat provides more contact between the valve and the seat and a better transfer of heat from the valve to the seat. "The exhaust seat gets pitted over time," adds Lee, "and the wider seat also means the valve job will last longer."

4. Lee finishes by lapping the valve into the seat with valve lapping abrasive. The lapping is a good

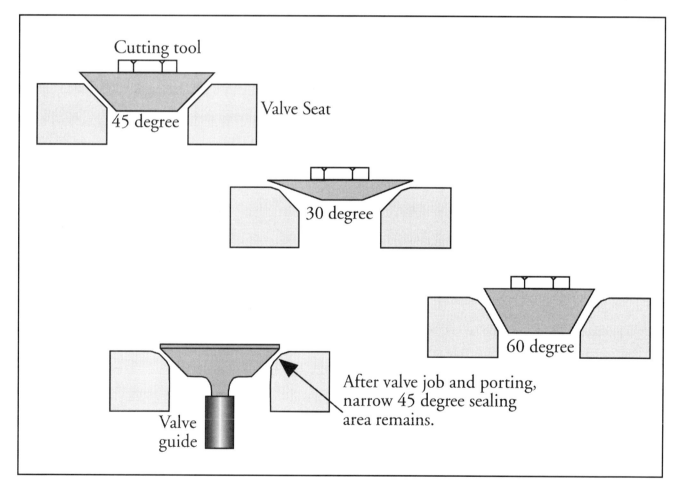

This simple illustration shows how the sealing area is moved up or out, during a good porting operation. And how the diameter of the seat can be increased as a result.

way to finish off the valve job (it eliminates any high spots that might exist on the seat or valve) and it also leaves the imprint of the seat on the valve making it possible to see exactly how close to the edge the sealing surface actually is.

PORTING AN EVO

When it comes to a pair of factory Evo heads, the real gains in airflow come from grinding work done to the seat and bowl area below the seat. The cross section through the bowl should be about the same size as the diameter of the valve. Lee also checks the size of the bottom of the valve seat insert against the valve diameter, this should end up at about 85 to 88 percent (opinions differ) as big as the diameter of the valve.

Lee starts the porting work by modifying the short side radius (the "short" corner between the seat and the edge of the head) and blending the edge where it meets the seat. Then he works around the edge of the seat. The idea is to blend the area where the seat meets the head casting, (there is often a ledge there as the seat insert is a smaller diameter than the casting) and increase the diameter of the seat just below the sealing area. Though it's an oversimplification, the idea is to make it easy for the air to move through the port and into the cylinder

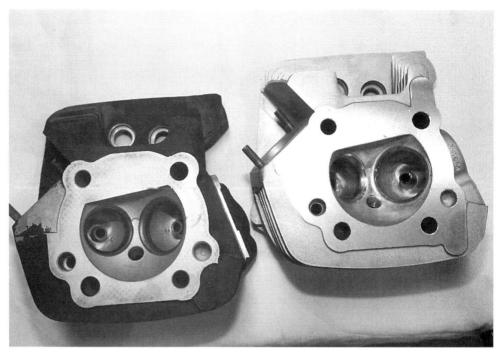

With Evo heads, much of the porting work is done in the bowl, under the valve seat, so the differences between stock (on the left) and ported are harder to see.

Notice the lack of sharp edges and how the port evolves into the seat. The bowl needs to be a specific size relative to the valve for optimal airflow.

105

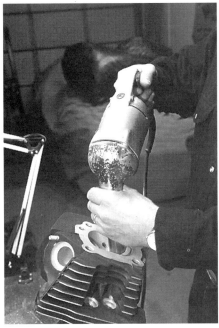

Port a TC: Step one at Lee's is to use a grinder to create a relatively wide 45 degree surface.

Next Lee starts to define the sealing area with the cutters, which come in various angles.

After using the 30 and 60 degrees cutters Lee has a nice narrow sealing surface for the exhaust valve.

without encountering any rough edges or restrictions that inhibit flow.

Most of the real grinding is done with a coarse carbide burr, then finished with a finer carbide burr

and finally a series of sand-paper rolls and "flappers." Intake ports are final finished with a sanding roll, then a flapper equipped with a piece of 60 or 80 grit paper. The exhaust ports are more highly

On this TC head the porting starts as Lee runs a marker around the inner edge of an exhaust gasket.

Lee will remove material up to that edge just drawn on the port.

Most porting work isn't this obvious, note the difference in size between the before and after exhaust ports.

polished, in which case Lee uses 240 grit paper as the final step.

The description above describes a Super Street porting job. Lee also offers a Pro Street Evo porting operation that uses a slightly larger intake valve. A stock Evo flows about 130 CFM measured at ten inches of water (more later), the Super Street porting job will boost that figure to 155 CFM at .600 inches of lift.

PORTING A TWIN CAM

Though the Twin Cam is a better engine than an Evo in many ways, there is this one little problem with the heads, at least as viewed from a performance perspective. That problem is the amount of air the stock heads will flow. While a stock Evo flows 130 CFM at ten inches of water, a pair of stock Twin Cam heads only flows 125 with the same lift measured on the same flow-bench. The simple answer might be a porting job, but as Lee describes it, even the porting work is more difficult. "Not only is the exhaust valve smaller, the exhaust port is visibly smaller than on an Evo. So it takes quite a bit more time on a Twin Cam head, as compared to an Evo, to get the same level of improvement."

Like the Evo, Lee offers Twin Cam heads in two different stages: What Lee calls a stock ported head with a stock intake valve and a stock exhaust valve, or the Pro Street porting job that uses bigger intake *and* exhaust valves.

When it comes to the actual porting of the Twin Cam heads, Lee reports that unlike the Evo which tends to benefit mostly from improvement of the seat and the area just under the seat, the Twin Cams need help all the way through the port. "Superflow says the biggest losses are from expansions in the port," says Lee. "Because the air flow slows down there. I take out a lot of material on either side of the valve guide in order to make the cross section of the port constant all the way, especially on the exhaust port."

The careful massaging of the Twin Cam ports results in a head that flows 160 CFM at ten inches of water with a .600 inch lift cam, as opposed to 125 for a stock head under the same conditions.

When a customer asks which of the Twin Cam heads is best for their bike, Lee asks them, "What kind of horses are you looking for, and is it a heavy bike like a Bagger?" He goes on to explain that, "To get over 100 horses (this assumes a 95 cubic inch motor), you need the bigger valves. But if you're riding a Bagger, you probably won't be turning the same rpm, and the somewhat smaller valves give more torque."

TC Porting continued: The intake port is opened up here, but not as much as the exhaust.

Like the Evo head work, the seat area needs to be a specific size relative to the valve.

Here you see Lee take as he works to enlarge the area under the seat and blend it into the bowl.

More TC Porting: Here we see Lee massaging the ports. His "Dremel tool" is cable driven.

This sand paper roll is used as one of the finishing steps. Exhaust ports get a more highly polished finish.

Lapping in the valve is the last step, designed to ensure he still has a well defined sealing surface.

Valves, R to L: Stock TC and EVO int. O-size int., used on TC. Stock TC exh. 1.565 in. Stock EVO exhaust 1.610 in. Aftermarket exh. typically used on the TC. 1.615 in.

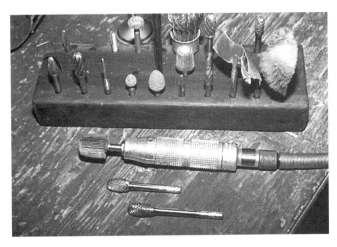

Lee's tool of choice, a cable driven grinder with carbide bits, stones, sand paper rolls and flappers in various "grits."

THE FLOW BENCH
The SuperFlow 110 & 600

Before the flow bench work can start, Lee explains that, "You need to make the tests with the head on a cylinder that's the same size (within 1/8 inch) as the cylinder the head will be used on. I use an intake manifold and velocity stack on the head when I check intake ports."

Lee runs all his tests at 10 inches of water, as measured on the column on the left of the flow bench. Across the top we see the actual flowmeter, which reads percentage of flow. The total CFM the machine will flow varies depending on how many of the orifices are left open at the top of the machine.

Lee methodically tests each port at a series of valve openings and then with no valve at all. The readings are taken as a percentage of flow number, which is then converted to actual CFM through a series of calculations.

The worksheet Lee does on each head is extensive and contains a wealth of information for the experienced mechanic. Among the calculations that Lee does is the percentage difference between what the intake will flow and what the exhaust will flow. The exhaust should flow 75 percent or more of what the intake will flow (with its bigger valve).

"When I look at my CFM numbers," says Lee. "I'm comparing them against other numbers that I have obtained on my flow bench. I'm careful about calibrating my machine and filling out the worksheets, so my numbers today are comparable to flow readings I took a year ago. But there are a lot of variables between machines and methods, even if they are both run at 10 inches of water, so you have to be careful when comparing the figures of different shops."

Lee reports that any good porting shop will have a flow bench to document their work, and that you should get a copy of the worksheet when you pick up the heads, so you know exactly how much they improved as a result of all that grinding. New to Lee's shop is a model 600 Superflow, that operates at 25 inches of water instead of 10. With the larger scale and increased capacity, small changes in flow are easier to see, as is turbulence in the port.

Lee's final words on flow benches: "You've got to have one to do any porting work. There is no other way to know what you're doing. I could have made the Twin Cam port look real nice and it still wouldn't flow any more than the stock one. But with a flow bench you know what works and what doesn't."

SuperFlow 600 allows flow to be checked at 25 inches of water, as measured by the manometer on left. Smaller manometer measures percentage of flow.

Fixture on the head with dial indicators is used to open each valve a specific amount so flow can be checked at various openings. Velocity stacks emulate carburetor and exhaust pipes.

80 Inches or More?

Combinations that Work

This chapter is intended to act as a guide to anyone hopping up an 80 cubic inch Evo. The chapter is divided up into two sections: One is intended for riders wishing to keep the stock displacement and the other is meant to provide guidance and tips for anyone thinking of increasing the bore or stroke of their 80 inch EVO-style engine. While monster motors get all the press these days, there's nothing wrong with a good strong 80-inch Evo, especially when you take a look at what it

Riders who want more displacement but don't want to bore the cases for bigger jugs should consider this Hot Set Up 89 from S&S. 4-5/8 inch flywheels bump the displacement while the pistons provide a compression ratio of 9.25 to 1. Complete with the right choice for camshaft, adjustable pushrods and E or G carb.

costs to increase the displacement or buy a complete big-bore motor.

Most of us have to live within a budget. The least expensive hop ups are generally those that retain the 80 cubic inch displacement. An increase in displacement means buying cylinders and pistons and/or a stroker flywheel assembly. Unless you're a fairly good mechanic, it also means paying someone else to do all or part of the engine assembly.

With engines of over 100 cubic inches available as complete units, it might seem the days of stroker cranks and "Sidewinder kits" are over. That for just a little more than the cost of what is essentially a complete engine overhaul with new flywheels and/or barrels and pistons, you can have a complete engine.

When I checked, a new 107 or 113 inch engine from S&S or TP Engineering sells for about $6000.00. A little less, a little more, depending on whether or not it's polished. Kokesh, a local aftermarket shop with a good reputation, tells me it's about half that to install a stroker kit in a stock Evo. That includes all the labor.

The nice thing about retaining the stock engine cases is the fact that you also retain the stock title with original engine numbers. The bike remains 100% Harley-Davidson with no need to create a new or modified title. In most cases

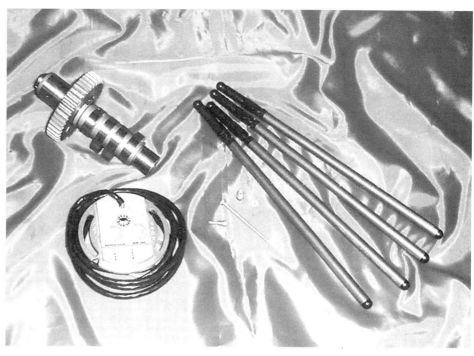

The System 75 has the potential to produce 75 horses and 75 foot pounds of torque and is a good choice for riders who don't want to pull the heads or do major engine work. Head Quarters

If you ask 10 good V-Twin mechanics which exhaust system produces the best mid-range power, 9 of them will recommend a two-into-one like this Pro Pipe from V&H.

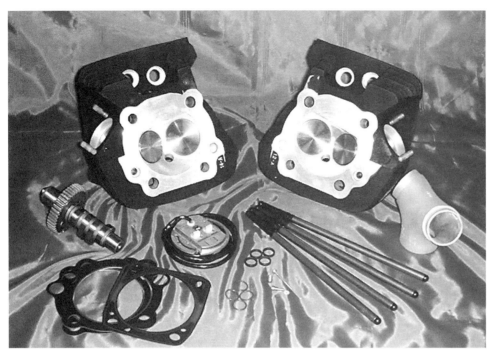

System 85 from HQ is designed as the half-way point between the rather mild 75 and high output 95. The combination of re-worked heads, stock pistons and HQ 0029 cam nets 9.5 to 1 compression, a good choice for heavier bikes. Head Quarters

you also retain an engine that looks stock, which makes the bike a sleeper at the stop-light Grand Prix.

THE RIGHT COMBINATION UNLOCKS THE POWER

This has all been said before, but we will say it again: There is no silver bullet. Good power comes through the use of components that work well together. You can't, for example, put a high lift cam in a bike with stock heads and valve springs. First, that cam probably only works well at higher RPM in an engine with more compression. And even if you spin the engine real fast there isn't enough spring pressure to keep the lifter rollers following the cam lobes.

V-Twin engines are more complex than the basic Chevy small block. That small block doesn't have any trouble with valve to valve clearance, or the collision of one piston with another when the stroke is changed. Building or modifying nearly any engine requires common sense, experience and TLC. Because of the design and the enormous number of possible combinations, building a good V-Twin requires extra amounts of all three.

So it all comes back to planning. How much power do you want, how do you intend to use that power and how much

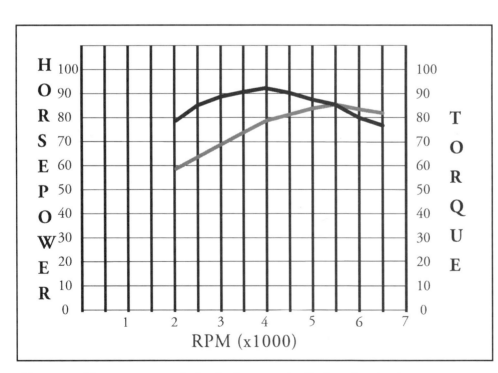

Torque and horsepower graph for the System 85 tells the tale: Good consistent horsepower starting as low as 2000 rpm with more than 80% of peak torque available at the same low RPM. Head Quarters

does the bike weigh? To quote long-time drag racer and Harley mechanic Lee Clemens from Departure Bike Works: "Each piece of the performance package, the carb, cam, exhaust pipes and heads is extremely critical. They have to be looked at as one mass. You have to consider them together because each one affects the others."

SECTION ONE, 80 INCH EVOS

You can get a Evo style engine to 70 or more horsepower pretty easily, without removing the heads. This is what we call a mild hop up, one that includes a cam change, new air cleaner and exhaust, and possibly an ignition upgrade.

With this kind of hop up you don't have to add compression or port the heads to realize significant gains in power. Note the interview with Doug Coffey from Head Quarters and the power gains that his shop is able to realize on an engine that retains the stock cylinder heads.

What does change on the mild hop ups is the camshaft, which necessitates a set of adjustable push rods, (check out the camshaft installation in the Chapter Seven). and the exhaust, which most riders change anyway. Because of the new cam and exhaust, it's necessary to rejet the carburetor so it can deliver the correct air-fuel ratio under the new conditions.

This is what a number of companies call their "Stage I" program. The key parts are the new camshaft, one that doesn't need new heavy-duty springs, and better breathing through the use of a new air cleaner and new exhaust.

If you have the stock staggered dual exhaust on your bike, you might consider retaining the stock header pipes and installing new slip-on mufflers instead of a complete new exhaust. Though many riders don't like the stock pipes with the cross-over pipe, the system is quite efficient, especially when equipped with a pair of less restrictive mufflers.

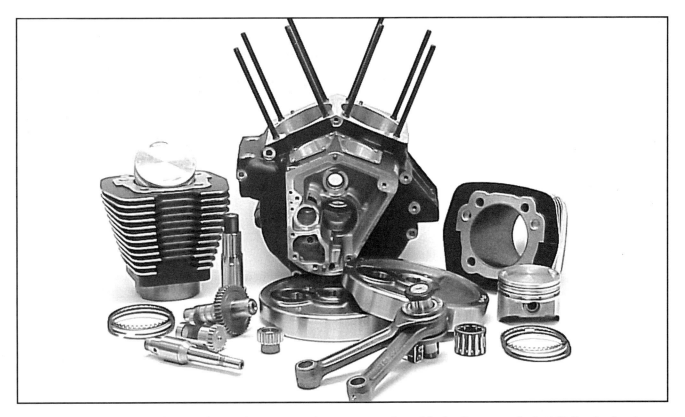

If you're worried about boring the stock cases, try this EVO-88 short block. Comes with 4-1/4" flywheel ass'm and 3-5/8" cylinders from S&S as well as your choice of two Red Shift cams depending on weight and riding style. Supply your own heads and oil pump. Zipper's

Light My Fire

HOW TO MAKE A SPARK

First, a brief look at how a basic ignition system works.

A coil is really nothing more than a transformer made up of two sets of wire windings, primary and secondary. If the coil is wired into a simple points-style ignition system current runs from the ignition switch to the positive terminal on the coil, through the primary windings, out the negative terminal and then on to the points. If the points are closed the current flows through them to ground. This current moving through the coil's primary windings creates a magnetic field which surrounds the coil. When the points open the current in the primary circuit is interrupted, which causes the magnetic field to collapse onto the secondary windings.

As you no doubt recall from Science class or Physics 101, when a magnetic field passes over a conductor a small current is induced in the wire.

In the coil a strong magnetic field passes over thousands of "wires," resulting in a sharp voltage rise within the secondary windings. In essence, primary current of just a few amps and 14 volts is transformed into a 30,000 volt spark with amperage measured in miliamps.

Suddenly opening a pair of points while current travels through them would normally result in an arc at the points. By installing a condenser of the right capacity in parallel with the points, the arcing of the points is minimized - and secondary output from the coil is increased as well.

You're still left with the basic problems of any point-style ignition system. Namely that the rubbing block is always rubbing, and wearing, changing the timing and reducing ignition output. Problem number two is the fact that the points themselves become pitted and dirty thereby reducing current flow in the primary side and output on the secondary side. The final drawback is the mechanical advance unit used with points-type ignition systems, which tends to be less precise and harder to adjust than the modern ignition curves pre-programmed into the various ignition modules.

In nearly all modern vehicles the points have been replaced by some type of electronic pickup. Most modern vehicles, including factory Evo-style Harley-Davidsons, have replaced the points with a hall effect or magnetic sensor which is often connected to the ignition

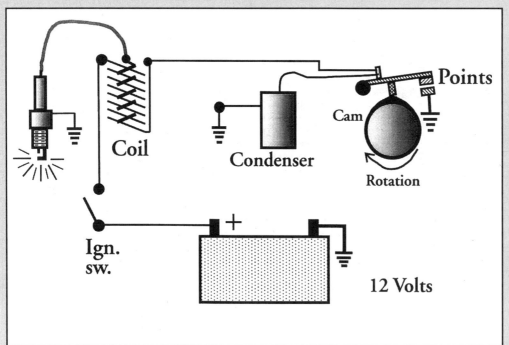

A very basic ignition system as might be used to provide spark for an old single-cylinder engine. Modern systems have replaced the points with a pickup that senses TDC as the engine turns.

Light My Fire

module. By replacing the points with some kind of sensor you eliminate the multiple problems of worn rubbing blocks and pitted points.

Now instead of the points opening as the piston nears TDC, the pickup "senses" the rotor as it spins by and signals the module to open the primary circuit.

Factory V-Twins use an ignition module to advance the spark, based on rpm and whether or not the VOES (vacuum operated electrical switch) is open or closed. This VOES is normally open under acceleration and conditions of low vacuum and closed during idle and cruise, or high vacuum, conditions. Each factory module has two advance curves, a faster curve for optimum conditions and a slower curve with less advance to minimize pinging under heavy load conditions. In this way low vacuum conditions signal the module to use the "retarded" curve.

AFTERMARKET SYSTEMS

All ignition systems use a primary and a secondary side. Differences in the aftermarket systems include the type of sensor used to provide timing information, whether or not the system uses a module, how they control the ignition advance, and whether or not a VOES switch is used. If your bike still has the factory ignition in place all you have to do is replace the module with a new one from the factory or aftermarket. Chose one that provides a faster advance curve, or a series of curves one of which is sure to match almost any engine configuration and riding style. New modules are available from Screamin' Eagle, as well as Dyna, Crane and others in the aftermarket. Most will plug right into the factory harness for plug-and-play simplicity.

Other systems like the popular HI-4 from Crane eliminate the module all together. These ignitions combine the sensor and "module" into one unit that fits under the nose cone. All you need is the unit under the nose cone and the coils.

Coils need to be chosen in conjunction with the needs of the ignition. The Crane system for example requires coils with at least 2 ohms of primary resistance. Pick high quality coils matched to the needs of the ignition, and compatible with the bracket on your bike.

If you are building a complete engine or want to start from scratch with a new ignition, complete ignition kits with coils and plug wires are available in all the catalogs from a number of well known companies.

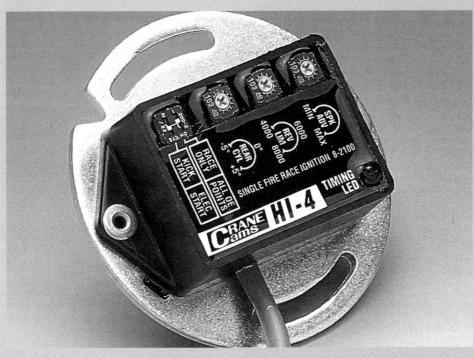

Among the most popular of the newer self-contained ignition systems is the HI-4 from Crane. Available in dual or single-fire models, this system does not need a separate ignition module. CCI

Light My Fire

The coil, whether a single fire like this or a dual fire, needs to have the right resistance for the rest of the system. CCI

Stock type ignition systems use an ignition module, which can be replaced with one like this with a faster ignition curve. CCI

SINGLE AND DUAL FIRE

Factory V-Twin ignition systems and many aftermarket ignitions operate in what is known as dual-fire mode. That is, the coil fires both spark plugs at the same time. When one cylinder is near TDC on the compression stroke and ready for the power stroke, the plug on that cylinder fires, at the same time the other cylinder also fires. The spark in the "other" cylinder is known as the waste spark. Specifically, when the front cylinder fires the rear cylinder is at 10 degrees ATDC; and when the rear cylinder fires the front cylinder is at 80 degrees BTDC. These figures assume 35 degrees timing advance.

In theory it would be more efficient to fire each plug alone, called single fire, and the more sophisticated ignitions do exactly that. When the front cylinder comes up to TDC that spark plug, and only that spark plug, fires. Most before-and-after dyno tests show little or no direct increase in horsepower. The switch to single-fire ignition always seems to result in a smoother running engine as judged by seat of the pants testing, however.

Not so Mild

To get beyond roughly 75 horsepower requires more compression. This can be obtained by milling the head or adding new higher compression pistons. If the engine is a high-mile unit, or you want to bump the displacement anyway, then replacing the pistons makes a lot of sense. If, however, you're happy with the 80 inch V-Twin and don't need new pistons or rings, you might want to have the heads shaved and possibly ported.

As always, there's more than one way to increase the compression. Each method has its proponents. At least one Harley shop I know of likes to use a higher compression Wiseco piston to get the ratio exactly where they want it while leaving the head alone (except for the porting on the higher output engines). At Donnie Smith's shop however, mechanic Don Tima commonly takes .050 inches or more off the head's sealing surface to increase the compression. How much he takes off generally depends on the camshaft he's installing. When I decided to install an EV 27 Andrews cam in my old Bagger, it was the representative from Andrews who told me how much to have milled off the head.

Sometimes the way in which the compression is raised depends on the application. Among the kits from Head Quarters, the 9.5

Another example of the integrated approach to hop ups, this System 95 is designed for light weight bikes and uses 10.5 to 1 compression, a 0023 HQ camshaft, and re-worked heads to achieve 95 horses from 80 cubic inches. Head Quarters

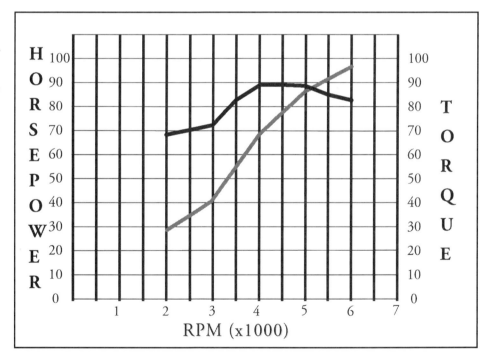

As engine builders and buyers get more sophisticated, more and more builders offer dyno charts on their various engine packages. Take a long look not just at total power, but the actual shape of the two curves. Head Quarters System 95 chart

Designed as an affordable Evo performance package, the 80/80 takes a stock 80 incher to 80+ rear wheel horsepower. The kit includes Stage II headwork with stainless valves, spring kit and pushrods, cylinder sizing with KB pistons, Red Shift 559 cam and Zipper's modified CV carb. Zipper's

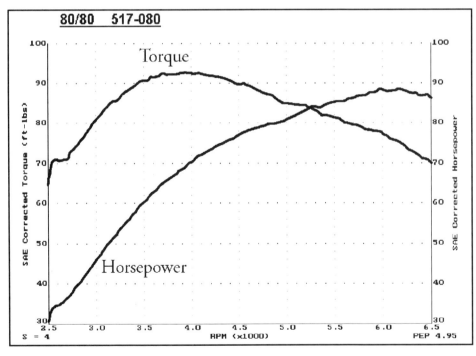

When the test Dyna was equipped with a Dyna ignition and Thunderheader the 80/80 kit produced nearly 90 horses and over 90 foot pounds of torque, with much of the torque available in the rpm range where most of us ride. Zipper's

to 1 kits retain stock pistons and rely on a little head shaving for the compression boost. Higher compression kits use heads with the same amount of material removed from the sealing surface, but add a piston with more dome volume to make up the difference.

A good mechanic or shop, working from experience, can pick a good combination of cam, carb and head modifications that will provide the power you want in the RPM range where you spend most of your time. Experience also means the mechanic knows how to set up the head for each camshaft that is commonly used. Unpleasant valve-to-valve, or valve-to-piston encounters are avoided in this way. For more on actual combinations check out the interviews with well-known engine builders in this book.

SECTION TWO, MORE THAN 80 CUBIC INCHES

If roughly 90 horses isn't enough, or you want substantial gains in torque than only more cubic inches can provide, or you simply want bragging rights, then you need more than 80 cubic inches.

You can increase the bore, the stroke or both. Like everything else, each strategy has advocates and detractors. Big-bore proponents like the way short stroke (relatively speaking) engines rev quicker and don't experience the high piston speeds sometimes seen with stroker engines.

And of course the stroker fans talk torque, torque, torque. Yes, they say, pistons speeds are higher, but it doesn't matter because you don't need to rev these motors as fast to get the same amount of power. In the end the choice is yours, based on your bike, the type of riding you do and the advice you get from your favorite shop or mechanic.

INCREASE THE BORE

To increase the bore you need new cylinders and pistons. In order to install new cylinders with larger bores the cases must be machined to accept the larger diameter spigots (the bottom section of the cylinder). Obviously you can only take this process so far before the case is seriously weakened, especially on the right side. Factory cases are not all the same in terms of strength (see Rob Carlson's comments that follow). Shops with expe-

rience recommend an increase to only 3-5/8 inches, from the stock 3-1/2, particularly if your engine was manufactured between 1989 and 1995. Aftermarket cases are generally stronger and can be punched out all the way to 3-13/16 for a total of 97 cubic inches when combined with a stock 4-1/4 inch flywheel assembly.

BUILD A STROKER

A stroker is just that, an engine with a longer-than-stock stroke. Instead of the stock 4-1/4 inch dimension the stroke is increased to 4-5/8 inches or more. The S&S stroker kits with a 4-5/8 inch dimension are very popular. By combining a stock 3-1/2 inch bore with the 4-5/8 inch stroke the displacement is increased to 89 cubic inches. Kits that take the stroke all the way to 5 inches are also available. Each increase in stroke provides more displacement and the potential for more torque and horsepower – as well as more vibration.

When ordering a big-bore kit be sure the piston weights are close to stock to avoid the hassle of rebalancing. S&S

BIG-BORE OR STROKER?

For a better look at this whole business of increasing the displacement, and the various costs and pitfalls of each method, we had a short conversation with Rob Carlson, co-owner of Kokesh MC located outside Minneapolis, Minnesota. With many years of experience Rob is able to shed some light on the murkier aspects of stroker and big-bore kits.

"Well, a stroker is better if you're using standard factory cases, because the right side of that case, the cylinder base by the front tappet block, is a little thin. We've seen a lot of cases break in that area, even when the owner only went to a 3-5/8 inch bore. Among all the factory cases the weakest ones seem to date from 1989 up to about 1995.

"If you're going to do a big bore kit it might

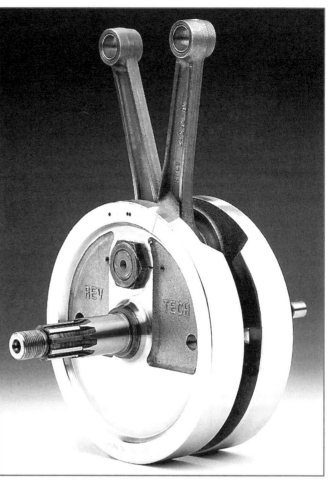

Many of the new flywheel assemblies use one-piece wheels and shafts, like this assembly from a complete RevTech 100 cubic inch V-Twin. CCI

Left side view of the new RT engine shows the tightly packed cooling fins, designed to promote cooling and eliminate hot spots. CCI

be a good idea to use aftermarket cases. But then there's the title issue. It's no longer a stock Harley engine with Harley numbers. You will have to tell the state about the engine and have the stock title amended.

As Rob goes on to explain, the stroker kit is generally less expensive, even if you don't buy aftermarket cases as part of the big bore kit. Prices quoted here are approximate and may not include every gasket. Remember too that labor rates differ widely from shop to shop and from one part of the country to another.

"In our shop a stroker kit is about two thousand dollars installed. You're basically rebuilding the whole motor, so that includes the labor to R&R the engine, do the complete rebuild, clearance the cases for the new 'wheels and re-balance the crank assembly. The parts include the stroker 'wheels from S&S with the sprocket shaft and new pistons. In our shop the two thousand would allow enough money for a new camshaft too. Some people do a port and flow job on the heads at the same time but that's extra of course. Personally, I like the 89 cubic inch engines with the 4-5/8 inch stoke. That's a safe kit to install and it's still something you can definitely feel in terms of the extra power.

By combining a stroker flywheel with 3-5/8 inch cylinders bore, displacements from 96 to 103 cubic inches are possible. S&S

"For a big-bore kit we charge about three thousand dollars if you use the stock cases. The labor is pretty much the same whether you install a stroker kit or big-bore kit. With the big bore kit you have to machine the cases for the larger cylinders. You should re-balance the crank while it's apart because you're adding new pistons. The biggest difference in the two prices is the cost of the kits. The big-bore kit costs a lot more than the stroker kit. If you decide to add aftermarket cases then you have to add another nine hundred dollars to the total cost.

The prices discussed above do not include the cost of a new carburetor. According to Rob, "you can run the stock carb, or something like an S&S E if you already have that on your bike, up to about 96 cubic inches, that's the cut off. After that you probably want to go to a S&S G or the new

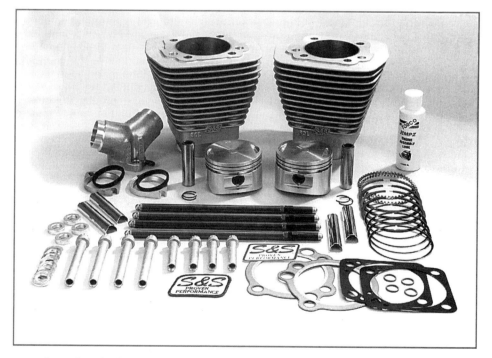

Big-bore fans looking for more cubes without an increase in stroke can buy 3-5/8 inch cylinders and pistons (cast or forged) in a complete set. Includes head bolts and all necessary gaskets. S&S

bigger Keihin or something similar."

"For value I think the stroker is a better deal. What might be the best deal for the money though is what we call our port-and-flow job. This includes port and flow the heads, a new cam, rejetting the carburetor, and all the labor. That only costs about fifteen hundred dollars without pipes or a carburetor. Depending on the cam you end up with 83 to 90 horsepower.

INTERVIEW, DOUG COFFEY FROM HEAD QUARTERS

The aftermarket is filled with shops and manufacturers who specialize in extracting more power from both Evo and Twin Cam engines. Among all those shops both large and small, there is a Canadian company by the name of Head Quarters with a reputation for assembling good "combinations." Combinations that include just the right heads, cam, carb and ignition to make great power without sacrificing ride-ability. The man who figured out those combinations is Doug Coffey, a rider and Harley wrench for over thirty years. A man with some interesting views on what makes a V-Twin really rock.

Doug, how about some background on you?

Well, I started riding in 1966 as soon as I got my license. I was interested in choppers and in 1969 I started a business selling chopper parts. By the mid-1970s I was still selling parts, but focusing more on custom painting. And then about 1978 S&S brought out the Side Winder kits. I was the first kid on the block to have one, that

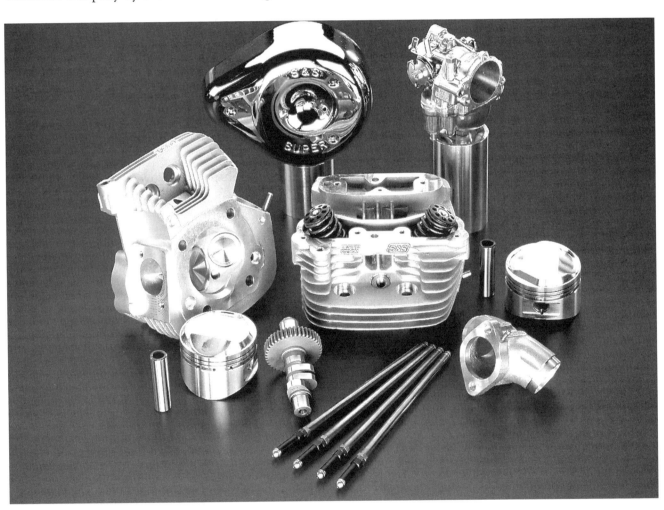

This 80FLSS Hot Set Up will provide more bang from your current Evo by increasing breathing and efficiency. Can be ordered in 10 to 1 or 11.6 to 1 compression, comes with heads and matching pistons, appropriate camshaft, adjustable pushrods and a E or G carb. S&S

engine worked and it didn't blow up. So from that point on we were doing a lot of motor building.

In 1980 or 1981 I was looking for something that would keep us busy all year 'round, through the winter months. We went into distributing parts with lines like James gaskets, Primo parts and engine components from S&S. The wholesale did so well that pretty soon I closed the retail store. In about 1987 I kind of got back into doing motors again. I bought a flow bench and thought I would offer head service to Canadian dealers so they wouldn't have to send all their heads to California.

One thing led to another and I made a couple of discoveries. One was bathtub Shovelheads. I called Hot Bike and they suggested I write a story,

so I did and eventually became a contributor to Hot Bike. I did one article every other month. The response to the articles was so great I thought I should advertise our products and services. And that's when Head Quarters spread our wings into the US and the rest of the world.

Tell us where Head Quarters is now, what is the biggest part of your business?

We are focused on reworking factory Harley heads, which I believe are the best heads on the market. Those heads give us the best end results. We also make cams, valve guides and ignitions. People ask why we don't make our own heads. The reason is simple, we can't make a better head than the factory does.

What makes those heads so good?

Even the high-dollar customs often utilize nothing more than a leaned-on 80 inch V-Twin, dressed out with the latest accessories, to get down the road.

They are very well designed. We are able to clean up the castings, which is labor prohibitive for the factory. With the bolt-on heads that are so popular, they simply cast a bigger port. Consequently the stock heads have smaller cc ports. We are able to get the same flow from a smaller port, so we get better velocity than you do with a bigger port in an aftermarket head.

You offer various hop-up kits for Evos. Can you describe the kits and the best application for each one?

I am a firm believer that heavy bikes and bikes with taller gears should not have over 9.5 to 1 compression. So we have developed a kit for the Evo and another for the Twin Cam that will give them 9.5 to 1 compression. And then we have a cam that works with that compression and takes advantage of the porting but keeps high cylinder pressure. Note, these kits include cam(s), heads, pushrods and assorted gaskets and small parts.

For lighter bikes we have another kit that gets the compression to 10.5 to 1. I go back to muscle car days, the stout motors with high compression were always in the lighter cars.

At Arlen Ness you can order a kit like this one - in any of about a hundred variations. Pick both internal and external component, including powder coat or polish.

And for the budget guy we have a bolt-in kit. It's a bolt-in cam, adjustable pushrods, a jet and needle kit, and we recommend one of our ignitions.

I find that cylinder pressure is the name of the game. If I have a 9.5 to 1 kit I also have a cam that closes earlier to maintain cylinder pressure, I want 180 psi cranking pressure. If I use that same cam in a 10.5 to 1 engine the cylinder pressure is 200, so instead we close the valve later to bleed off some pressure.

My cams are always different than others in industry. My ramps are asymmetrical, the opening and closing ramps have different shapes. And they're double pattern, meaning the exhaust lobe has a different shape than the intake lobe.

It all revolves around gearing and weight. I get people who want to have more horsepower on a dresser. But I try to talk that person out of installing that high compression kit in a heavy bike.

What about exhaust, what do you like to see people use for exhaust? If you could have riders do a blind test they would all take Screamin' Eagle mufflers on stock header pipes with the cross over. My personal favorite is a 2 into 1 Supertrapp. I try to steer people away from drag pipes or 2 into 2 pipes.

V Thunder makes bolt-in cams that don't need any head modifications, as well as high-lift grinds that require careful checking by experienced mechanics.

Valve spring kits list the seat pressure and height for each set installed and open. As well as the coil bind dimension. Crane

When do they have to throw out the stock CV carb?

I don't think ever, at least not up to 95 cubic inches. And even then they don't have to if it's a taller geared, heavier bike. The larger carbs work better in the shorter geared, lighter bikes with bigger engines - when they want high end power, not low and mid-range torque.

I built a 98 cubic inch Dresser with a 9.5 to 1 engine. It made 100 horses at 6000 RPM on the dyno, with a 40mm Keihin constant velocity carb. I like CV carbs. We've had people put them back on after buying an aftermarket carb. We encourage people to use them. Part of the trouble is when the bike comes from the factory, the carb is jetted for the restrictive pipes and air cleaner. The owner will fix those two things, without touching the carb, and now the bike runs poorly and spits back out the air cleaner. So then they replace the carb.

We like to see them rejet and re-needle the CV because that's a pretty good carburetor. We don't like to see people drill out the hole in the slide piston and add the lighter spring. When people do that the piston moves too fast. We sell a lot of stock springs and stock pistons to fix carbs that are already modified.

You've got a 113 cubic inch engine in the catalog. Can you tell us a little about that?

The 113 is a motor assembled by Kendall Johnson, the man in charge of our operation in North Carolina. It's mostly S&S components all hand assembled and balanced. I port the heads, Kendall assembles the engine with one of our cams and our ignitions. It comes in three configurations, depending again on the gearing and weight of the bike the engine is going into. Kendall's strongest motor makes 130 horsepower and 130 foot pounds of torque.

Given the availability of these very powerful four-inch bore engines, does it make sense to spend money adding cubes to an Evo? And if you do add cubes, do you prefer to increase bore or stroke?

Well, everyone wants cubes, that's the thing. And if you're building a bike you have to consider

Adjusting the Valves

After talking with Doug Coffey we realized that what seems like a simple operation, adjusting the valves, is more complex that it first appears. As Doug explains, "It's important that people understand the hydraulic lifter. That lifter has a hydraulic plunger inside. Normally the

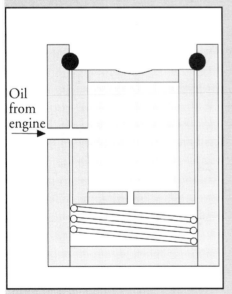

A simplified look inside a hydraulic lifter.

space under the plunger is filled with oil. What keeps the lifter in its bore is a snap ring."

"When you adjust the pushrod you are compressing the oil, but the oil won't compress so you are actually lifting the valve off it's seat. If, after adjusting the valves on one cylinder, you roll the engine over to adjust them on the other you can run the valves into the piston. More valves are bent in this way than any other.

"After adjusting the pushrods on one cylinder, it's a good idea to wait until those lifters are fully bled down before rolling the engine over. This can take as much as forty-five minutes. I always find something else to do until that happens. The final test is spinning the pushrod between my fingers. If it spins the lifter is bled down and you can roll the engine over. If the pushrod won't spin after forty-five minutes something is wrong.

resale. But I can make an 89 or 92 cubic inch Evo work as well as anything that's bigger and make it real reliable. I don't believe in the big bore. The best bang for the buck is a stroker motor, I like the 92 inch motors but that's not a kit deal. You could say I am pro stroke. If I only had to do one or the other I would add to the stroke.

How about the mistakes people make in buying and building motors?

The biggest mistake is they do everything too big, the ports, the cam and the carb. And they make the wrong ignition choices. For example, on Sportys, I believe in using stock cams and pushrods and 883 heads when we punch them out to 1200cc. Then we port the 883 heads and use 1200 valves which gives us a smaller combustion chamber so it has more compression and better quench. Now we add Screamin' Eagle mufflers and Head Quarters ignition and you've got the most horsepower per dollar you can achieve on a Harley. We see 90 horsepower and 90 foot pounds in these Sportsters. But people want big cams with adjustable pushrods and big ports. When they put it together they get 74 horsepower with tuning problems.

In terms of setting up the heads I find that the stock valve train geometry is perfect, you don't have a problem as long as you honor their valve-stem protrusion specifications. I've had guys trade up to a new bike and want to use the heads we did for them a few years back on the new bike. They send the heads to us for freshening and we see no measurable guide wear after sixty or seventy thousand miles. If we honor those factory service parameters we don't have any problems. People do get into trouble though. Some of the valves are manufactured to a dimension that's too long. And a lot of the cams are made so that in order to have the correct valve-to-valve clearance they must sink the valves into the seat, which means they probably have too much valve-stem protrusion. When you sink the valves too deep you get a shallow port, and you loose compression because the combustion chamber has more volume.

Why did you develop your own ignition?

There was nothing available that did the job right. The stock ignition starts at 5 BTDC and goes to 35 BTDC for a total of 30 degrees advance. A lot of people understand that when they increase the compression they need to retard the spark slightly. The problem is, with most ignitions, if you retard the timing you retard the whole window. The whole curve slides back 5 degrees. So now you start at TCD and go to 30 degrees. But what you really want is to start at 5 degrees and go to 30 for a total of 25 degrees. Ours does that. It doesn't make more power. All mine does is make them start easier and run through the curve happier.

Doug Coffey is a man who seems able to do well with whatever he chooses - be it custom painting, engine building, porting heads or designing camshaft profiles. The end result is sanitary motorcycles that run hard. Head Quarters

Complete Engines

Big Bore and More

If 80 or 89 cubic inches just won't do the job, then it's time to consider buying a complete aftermarket engine. Possibly one with a bore diameter of four or more inches. As described elsewhere, you can only push a standard Evo-style engine so far, in terms of increasing the displacement, before you run out of room in the case. Whether you can safely push the bore to 3-5/8 inches or more depends on which brand of cases you have and your tolerance for risky behavior. Even the best of the after-

S&S Super Stock 4 inch bore engines come complete with strokes of 4, 4-1/4 or 4-1/2 inches for displacements of 100, 107 and 113 cubic inches. S&S

Big-bore cylinder kits combine the super tough cast cylinders and high-nickel liners with TP's own forged pistons. Available from 3-1/2 to 4-1/8 inches. Hackett

and a few others are right behind. Most of these engines use a four-inch bore as the foundation that makes the big displacement possible. By combining a four-inch bore with a four, four and a quarter or four and a half inch stroke, displacements of 101, 107 and 113 inches result. And yes, even bigger bores are just around the corner.

To encompass the larger bore these cases use a larger stud pattern, and lifter bores that are positioned farther to the right, which then

market cases however, can be bored to only 3-13/16 inches.

To better explain these big-bore brutes we've included an interview with Tom Pirone from TP Engineering farther along in the chapter. Also included here is a short shop tour of the TP Engineering manufacturing facility.

HISTORY

This movement toward engines with bores of four inches or more really got started a few years back when S&S brought out a new set of cases, cylinders and heads, all designed around a four-inch bore cylinder. By combining the four inch bore with a stroke of four or more inches S&S was able to bring to market engines of 101, 107 and more cubic inches. In fairness we should also mention the fact that some smaller shops like Hyperformance in Iowa were building engines of 116 and more cubic inches, based on cases from STD and other manufacturers, well before these new complete offerings came to market.

Today there are a number of companies manufacturing complete engines with displacements that run to 120 and more cubic inches. We've already mentioned S&S, though TP Engineering, Merch

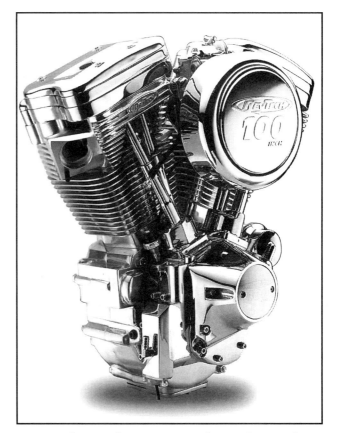

Among the complete engines on the market are these 88 and 100 cubic inch units from RevTech manufactured in an ISO 9000 manufacturing plant specifically for Custom Chrome. Features include reinforced cases, one-piece flywheel halves and O-ring head gaskets. CCI

King of Cubes

HYPERFORMANCE

Randy Torgeson, the owner and power behind Hyperformance, Pleasant Hill, Iowa, cut his teeth repairing and porting cylinder heads. That was in the early days, before he started manufacturing his own "Big Jugs" from ductile iron in bore sizes of four inches and more. The new nick name came as Randy began mating his cast iron cylinders with a stroker bottom end, installed in a set of STD cases. The resulting engine measured 116 cubic inches back in the days when a "96" was considered radical.

If you ask Randy why he likes cast iron cylinders, he says it's because they're both stronger and more stable dimensionally than aluminum. Because they don't grow as the engine warms up (at least not nearly to the degree aluminum cylinders do) there is no problem with running solid lifters. And a cylinder that started out perfectly round when the engine was cold, will still be perfectly round when it's at full running temperature.

These Big Jugs are available with or without fins for street or competition use. They can even be metallic coated for better aesthetics and matched up to round-fin cylinder heads from R&R.

You can "one up" your riding buddies and their 113 inch engines from S&S or TP with a 139 inch V-Twin assembled from 4-3/8 inch Big Jugs, a 4-5/8 S&S flywheel assembly and dual carb heads from R&R. The outer limits at Hyperformance include a 156 cubic inch engine created in cooperation with DÜX, a German motorcycle parts distributor, and an astonishing 179 cubic inch V-Twin!

At Hyperformance, the engines and parts don't come off an assembly line. Each one is very much a hand assembled deal designed for one particular customer. So when only the best, or the biggest will do, give a call to the King of Cubes.

One of Randy's smaller V-Twins is this 106 cubic inch package made up of Delkron cases and Hyperformance ductile iron Big Jugs with metallic coating, topped off with R&R billet heads.

Ductile iron Big Jugs are available in sizes that range from stock to 5-1/8 inches. Can be metallic coated for better visuals. Hyperformance

New on the scene is this 114 cubic inch Rev-o-lution engine. What is described as "a smooth high revving engine in an attractive traditional V-Twin styled package." Mid-USA

els, where most of us spend most of our time (note Tom Pirone's comments in the interview in this chapter).

WHAT TO BUY

If what you want is to replace the factory engine in your current bike, or buy a complete mill to power that bike-building project in the garage, then take the time to check out all the companies with complete engines for sale. Though we've focused on engines with a bore of at least four inch es, don't rule out engines like the two RevTech models with displacements of 88 and 100 cubic inches. In fact, as we go to press some Harley dealers still have new Evo engines for sale at very competitive prices, as well as complete TC Engines with or without the counter-balancers.

Whatever you buy, try to select a known engine from a known entity. Don't volunteer to be part of

requires a longer pinion shaft to match. What this means is that cases, cylinders and heads designed for use with engines with bores up to 3-13/16 can not be used with the new four-inch bore components.

Most of the companies in this market offer their complete engines in at least two stages of performance. S&S, for example, offers their 107 inch engine with either a 9.6 to 1 compression ratio for street use, or in a competition package that features Supreme rods, a hotter cam and a 10.7 to 1 compression ratio. Though we all want the fastest motor we can buy, it's often better to settle for the engine with lower compression and slightly less horsepower in the name of better day-to-day rideability.

We all want as much power as we can buy. But the engine with less than maximum output rewards you with better power at low and middle RPM lev-

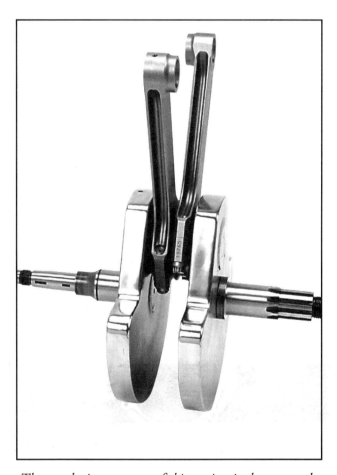

The revolutionary part of this engine is the unusual automotive-style crank assembly with offset Carrillo rods featuring plain bearings on the bottom end instead of the traditional rollers. Mid-USA

a R&D group testing a new combination of parts "guaranteed to make tons of horsepower." The huge number of companies making parts for the EVO-style engine, and the unlimited number of possible combinations that can be assembled into a running engine, mean that there are a tremendous number of shops and companies offering complete or nearly complete engines for sale. Drag racers and serious motorheads might enjoy trying different combinations of parts

S&S cases are cast from 356 aluminum, and come with Timken main bearing races installed and pinion shaft bearing race pressed in and line bored.

in the search for that perfect engine. The rest of us simply want lots of power in a package that can be used daily on the street.

Buy your engine complete or get the manufacturer's recommendation as to the which components (like the carburetor) is the best one to install on the engine. And plan to have a good mechanic or a "dyno shop" road test the bike when you get it running so the carburetor is sure to be dialed in correctly.

INTERVIEW: TOM PIRONE FROM TP ENGINEERING

One of the best things about the V-Twin aftermarket is the opportunity it provides individuals with a passion for motorcycles to actually manufacture better or sexier products for all the rest of us. Passion alone doesn't make a better product, however. It takes study and brains and experience and balls to truly make a better mousetrap.

Tom Pirone, owner of TP Engineering, is blessed with both the passion to build a great motor and the knowledge to actually proceed with a plan. So far that plan includes complete big-bore engines with enough power to pull the front wheel of a Road King off the ground at 2000 rpm in second gear. When you get him on the phone Tom will begin by telling you about his new design for pistons or connecting rods or some other

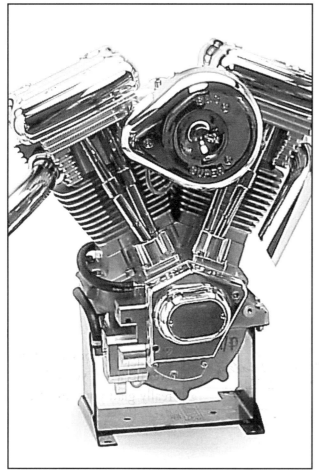

From Zipper's come complete torque-cruiser engines in 107 and 120 cubic inches. Both use a 4-1/4 inch stroke, matched with either a 4 or 4-1/4 inch bore. The 120 nets 140 foot pounds of torque. Zipper's

The Legal Press

KEEPING IT LEGAL

So that old 80 inch just won't do it anymore. Your friends are all riding aftermarket bikes with four-inch bore engines and it's time to step up. You call S&S and order a big-ass 113 cube mountain motor. When the motor arrives you just can't wait to get that new beauty stuffed into the frame rails and the bike back out on the road. At some point during or after the purchase of the motor you probably received a form, a MSO form, from the engine manufacturer. In your haste to get the engine installed and the running bike down to the local watering hole the MSO was probably left lying on the kitchen table or stuffed into a drawer. And now the bike is running so why bother with all that damned paperwork anyway?

WHY BOTHER

To get a handle on how, and why, it should be done (at least in Minnesota) we called resident bike builder Donnie Smith. As Donnie explains, "When you buy a motor you get a MSO for that engine. You have to take that to the deputy registrar, or wherever you buy your plates, and they have a form. You fill out the form and then they send out a letter. Then you have to take the bike and have it inspected. Eventually you get a new title that shows the new engine number. The only bad thing is, the new title is a reconstructed title, which I don't like but that's how they do it."

About why you should take this extra step, Donnie adds the following: "You don't have to do it, but then you might get in trouble later. Like in Sturgis or Daytona where they have those task forces looking for stolen bikes and checking all the frame *and* engine numbers."

So after spending hours installing the engine, tuning the carburetor and getting it running just right, spend another hour or two and do all the paper work. There might come some dark night along Atlantic avenue when you'll be really glad you did. And don't buy a motor without a MSO. If the deal seems too good to be true, or has that funny smell of fish left out too long in the sun, pass on it.

MANUFACTURER'S STATEMENT OF ORIGIN
MOTORCYCLE CRANKCASE

The undersigned, S&S Cycle, Inc. (the "Corporation"), hereby certifies that the new motorcycle crankcase described below, the property of the corporation, has been transferred   **May   16, 1995** on Invoice No.   086307   to: John's Cycle

       4334 Shady Lane

       Brandon, Mn 55555

       320-344-4411

CRANKCASE DESCRIPTION:

Trade Name:	SUPER STOCK	Year Mfg: 2001
Model:	31-0001	No. of Cylinders: 2
I.D. Number:	U 0915X	Case Weight (Dry): 23

The Corporation further certifies that this was the first transfer of such new motorcycle crankcase ordinary trade and commerce.

S&S PROVEN PERFORMANCE

S&S Cycle, Inc.
Box 215 Route 2 Hwy G
Viola, Wisconsin 54664

By: (Signature)   *Samuel L. Scaletta*
(Title)   Corporate Officer

FIRST ASSIGNMENT

FOR VALUE RECEIVED, the undersigned hereby transfers this Manufacturer's Statement of Origin and th motorcycle crankcase described therein to:

Name: _____

Address: _____

Each manufacturer has their own MSO. What's important is that you get one with the engine, and that any previous transfers are noted.

TP cases are cast from 356A aluminum and heat treated to a T-6 specification. Other then de-burring, all finishing operations are done on CNC equipment for accuracy and consistency. Hackett

These cylinders wait for boring and final finishing – done with diamond tipped tooling because, "the SP61 centrifugally cast high-nickel sleeve is so tough that boring takes too long when done with conventional tooling." Hackett

new project. Not because Tom likes to brag (he's one of the most modest people you're likely to meet) but because he's genuinely excited about the new piston or connecting rod.

With twenty years of experience building and manufacturing V-Twin engines, Tom is the perfect person to shed a little light on the care and feeding of an extra-large V-Twin engine.

Tom, let's start with some background on you and how you came to be an engine manufacturer.

I got involved out of the sheer love of the mechanics. Whether it's a Chevy smallblock or a Harley, I've been intrigued with the internal workings of an engine since I was a kid.

The reason I manufacture engines is two-fold. Part of the reason is supply and demand. We had a speed shop where we built performance engines with other people's components, but then in the early 1990s we couldn't get enough parts. The other half of the reason is the challenge of making a better part and ultimately a better engine. I wasn't going to shift gears from speed shop to engine manufacturer, unless I felt I could make the best one out there. That's what I'm trying to do. Our name stands for a premium product.

Do you manufacture all the parts that go into a TP engine?

It's taken time, but now we make everything except the cylinder head castings. Everything else is our own,

134

we even have our own rocker box covers and our own flywheel assemblies.

Tom, describe a couple of the parts you make yourself and specifically what you've tried to change or improve.

Well, on the flywheels, we've gone to a bigger 1-5/8 inch diameter pinion shaft, because as the cubes go up you have to provide more support for the flywheel assembly. And we have a new connecting rod. It's forged and machined so that the weight of each end is consistent, within one gram, from one rod to another. The consistent weight makes balancing easier and more precise. One of the other parts I'm really proud of is the new three-stage oil pump (on the pressure side). We actually received a patent on the oil pump.

There are more and more companies selling complete engines. How does a rider or bike builder pick a good engine, both in terms of quality and in terms of getting the right engine for a particular project?

If you are going to a big motor you have to do your homework. That means trying to decide which company has a good product and stands behind that product.

Technically, if what you want is a bigger engine and you're performance minded you must know two things. You have to know what you expect from the bike, and how it will be used. Will you ride this thing every day and fill it with pump-premium gas? Or is this the Sunday-only bike that runs on avia-

TP flywheels start as 4140 steel, chosen for its toughness and forgeabily, formed in a closed die forging operation. All machining and finishing operations are done on CNC equipment for consistent dimensions and weight. Hackett

Like the flywheels, the connecting rods are a closed-die forging made from 4140 steel. Rods are machined, internally and externally, on CNC equipment for consistent weight. Hackett

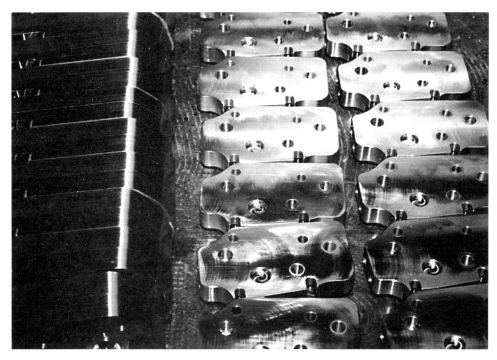

Oil pumps start as blanks of 6061 T-6 aluminum before being machined on CNC equipment.

tion gas and gets used on the drag strip occasionally? Is this a hot street bike or a drag strip bike?

Because there are two kinds of engines. The one that squeezes every possible horse out of the available displacement. And the other that will make good reliable power running on pump gas.

Once you've decided how the bike will be used, quiz the engine manufacturers. Will the engine you're looking at start reliably? Will it need compression releases, will it ping? Some engines are so close to the edge that you can't ride them on a hot summer day.

The motor you choose must match your riding style. Ask where it makes peak horsepower and torque. If you race you may want peak power at high RPM. For me, on a personal basis, low end torque is what puts a big smile on my face. Our engines make tremendous torque at 2000 RPM and don't run out of power until 5600 RPM. If you're going to the track you might want a high RPM motor. If you're around town you want low end torque, it's more fun.

How big should the motor be? When is a motor too big?

Well, the engine you buy must fit the frame, and it must fit your wallet. I've heard of guys who had a new frame with fresh paint and then their new engine wouldn't fit. Then what do you do?

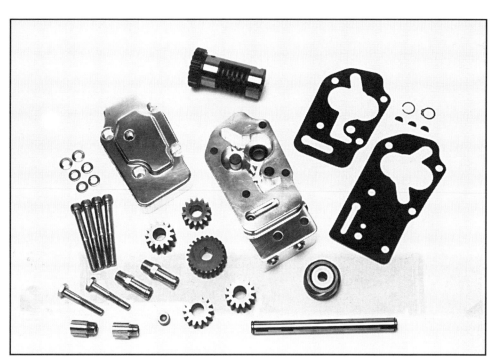

The TP Engineering oil pump started as a fresh sheet of paper and uses a three-stage pressure side controlled by self-contained stainless steel check valves. The design guarantees oil to the bottom end even at low rpm with hot oil. Hackett

For us, the 107 and 113 inch engines will fit in almost any frame. The 107 is a little shorter than an Evo-80, the 113 is the same height. The 116 is a little taller, and the new 121 is taller still.

What about component fitment on these big engines?

Everything that fits on the outside of an 80 inch engine will fit on one of the bigger engines. The only problem you might have is the exhaust. The cam cover is moved out one quarter inch which means some exhaust pipes that are real tight there might have to be dimpled to fit.

What about drivetrain issues with these big engines. Is a standard chain-style primary strong enough, what about the clutch and the final drive?

The chain primary is strong enough. Every bike I've built uses a primary chain. And I use a stock, wet clutch. As far as longevity goes the heavy duty clutches might last longer, I don't know. The final drive deal depends on the bike. If you've got a 130 series tire on a Road King, then the tire will break loose before the belt slips. But with a sticky 200 or 250 tire, the tire may hook up and then something's gotta give. But I do like to stay with a belt final drive, at least on my own bikes, because it's so clean.

What are the mistakes that people make when they buy these big-bore engines?

It's what I said before, they don't match the engine to their riding style. Or they don't match the rest of the components to the engine. I see riders who decided to buy the high-output high-compression engine, but didn't buy the big starter and the heavy duty battery. And they have trouble starting the engine and it isn't because the engine builder did anything wrong. It's a case of mis-matched components.

Each TP motor is blue-printed, "We check all the clearances, the ring gap, the cc of the heads, the cam end play...it's all checked and recorded." Hackett

Seen here with one of nine CNC centers in the building. Tom Pirone is a very hands-on engine designer and manufacturer. Hackett

Hands-On

Three Assembly Sequences

A COMPLETE ENGINE ASS'M @ ARLEN'S

Though most of us think of Arlen Ness as a bike builder and designer, his shop is also the source of an engine program designed to let the customer buy exactly the engine he or she desires.

A lot of shops and catalogs can sell you a big-inch engine or an engine with polished cylinder fins. But very few shops can sell you everything from an mild 80 inch Evo to a wild 120 inch Merch motor, each available with various parts polished or powder

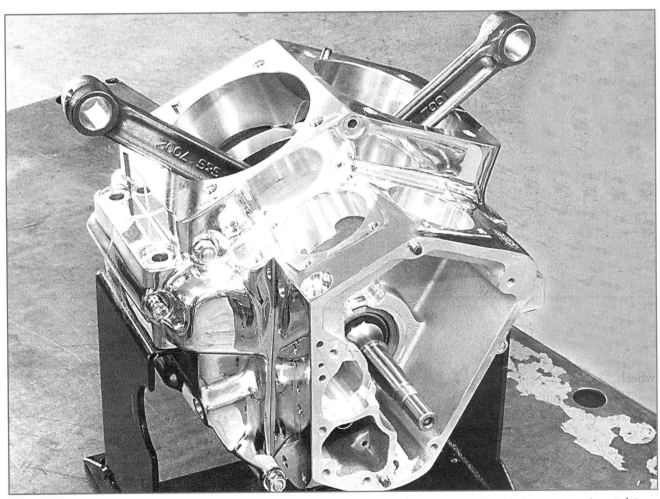

The 113 inch V-Twin being assembled at the Arlen Ness shop uses S&S 4-1/2 inch 'wheels, contained in S&S cast cases, mated to four-inch bore cylinders still to come.

coated in a wide range of colors. With the Arlen Ness engine program, you don't just get to choose camshafts or carburetors, you can pick the pushrods and even the brand of roller rockers you prefer. The order form, designed by Cory Ness, resembles a menu. Mix and match the components you desire, send it in and wait for a quote – usually only 24 hours.

To get a better look at the program we spent a few days in the Arlen Ness shop where Tony Birchfield assembled a 113 cubic inch S&S motor for an un-named customer.

This particular customer wanted polished cases, cylinders and heads. This required that the motor be shipped to Arlen's in pieces so Fernando Lopez could carefully polish first the cases and then the cylinders and heads. An experienced polisher, Fernando attends to the little things, like making sure the fins on the heads match up with the fins on the cylinders, simply because it looks so poor when the fins on one hang out farther than the fins on the other.

After unpacking the bottom end, the first job is to double check the work done at S&S in assembling the flywheels.

"We always put the wheels in the truing stand," explains Tony, "even though we've never really had any that were out of the specification. You just never know if one might be damaged in shipping for example."

In this case the specifica-

This simple fixture is the one used at Arlen's (and many other shops as well) to check flywheel runout.

These cases from S&S are numbered. The Timken bearings and spacer that came with the cases carry the same number. When installed the left side of the crank should have the correct end play.

139

The first job is to press the inner Timken bearing onto the flywheel shaft.

Now the case, then the spacer, then the outer Timken bearing are dropped in place.

With the correct tool Tony presses the outer Timken bearing into place.

tion calls for a maximum of .002 inches of runout at the shaft, as measured by the very simple fixture designed for just this and seen in the photo.

Once Tony knows the crank to be true, it's time to install the Timken bearings onto the left side of the flywheel assembly. The bearings and a spacer came in a small box marked with the same numbers written on the two case halves. "They set this up at S&S with their jigs," says Tony, "so the bearings are matched to the cases."

With the flywheels in a fixture Tony uses an installation tool to push the inner bearing down onto the base of the flywheel. Now the case can be set on to the bearing and the other, outer bearing pressed into place, with the spacer between the two bearings.

Now the right side roller bearing is slid onto the shaft followed by a snap ring.

Tony explains that when the crank is installed in the left side engine case there should be .0001 to .0005 inches of end play. "You should be able to move the individual rollers with a small screwdriver."

With the flywheel assembly installed in the left side case Tony can slide the right side roller bearing onto the shaft, with plenty of assembly lube, followed by the snap ring that holds the bearing in place. To seal the case halves he uses 1104 Threebond sealer available from the local auto parts store. "You can peel the excess sealer off and it doesn't leave a dark line or any of that" says Tony. With the right side case installed Tony can drop in the case bolts, after putting a little wax on the threads to prevent galling when the chrome bolts are mated to a chrome plated nut.

The case bolts are tightened to 20 foot pounds. After tightening the bolts Tony checks that item off the extensive check sheet that is part of every engine assembly at Arlen's.

Before installing the oil pump Tony plugs one of the two breather holes in the case with a pipe plug coated with sealer. S&S ships the cases with two holes, it's up to the installer to use one or the other depending on which better mates up to the frame. After putting a little Hylomar sealer on the oil pump gasket to hold it in place, Tony positions the gasket followed by the body of the oil pump.

Tony holds the oil pump gear in position as the pump is slipped into place, making sure the oil pump drive gear slips over the shaft as the pump is pushed up against the case. With wax on the threads Tony puts the two upper mounting bolts in snug before installing the key on the oil pump shaft, and the small snap ring that holds the key in place.

Now it's time to install the outer gasket and the remaining bolts, tightened according to the specifications in the service manual. The bolts are tightened gradually, and Tony makes it a point to ensure the pump turns freely as the oil pump bolts are brought to final torque.

With the oil pump in place it's time to install the drive gears for the oil pump and camshaft on the pinion shaft. First Tony slips the two keys onto the shaft, followed by the gear for the oil pump, then a spacer and finally the pinion. Note: pinion

With the roller bearing in place the right side case can be dropped in place (after applying the correct sealer to the mating surfaces).

Next the case bolts are installed and tightened evenly to the correct specification.

Among the parts that are laid out ahead of time are the new hydraulic lifters, the lifter blocks, breather gear, and the Crane cam with spacers.

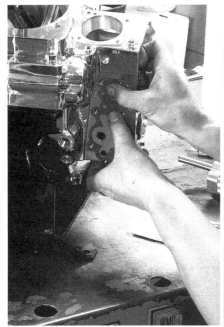

With a little sealer Tony sticks the oil-ump gasket to the case. Note the plug in the lower breather hole.

The oil pump is slipped into place while the gear is held in position inside the gearcase.

Here you can see the drive gear on the oil pump shaft and the key in place (harder to see) on the shaft.

shafts come in different configurations, straight and tapered, with one key or two. After putting red Loctite on the threads Tony screws the pinion nut onto the end of the pinion shaft. Final torque of the pinion-shaft nut is done with a torque wrench.

Installation of all the parts in the right side gearcase follows a specific sequence. With the pinion gear in place it's time to install the breather gear, which must be installed so it is timed correctly relative to the pinion gear, and with the correct amount of end play.

With a new gasket on the outer case and one of the small spacers in place on the end of the gear, Tony checks the clearance with a feeler gauge (check the photo here for clarification). The end spacers are available in various thicknesses and can be used to achieve a total end play of .001 to .010 inches with a used gasket in place. A new gasket will compress about .005 inches so the specification with a new gasket would be .006 to .015 inches.

Like the breather, the cam must be installed with just enough end play. In addition the fitment between the camshaft and the pinion gear must be just right.

To check the end play Tony pulls the breather gear out and sets it aside. Now he installs the cam

with both the thrust plate and a thrust washer in place on the end, followed by the cam cover and gasket.

After torqueing the bolts the actual end play is checked with a feeler gauge (a dial indicator can be used here as well), the specification Tony likes is .001 to .015 inches.

For fitment between the cam gear and the pinion gear, Tony explains that, "we used a red pinion gear, (pinion gears of slightly different sizes are available and can be identified by a drop of color on the gear) and Crane cuts their cam gears so they will mesh correctly with the red gear." Note: it's still a good idea to check the fitment between gears, in more than one location, as described in the other installation sequences.

Once the cam end play is right and Tony is happy with the fitment between the cam and pinion gears he can pull off the cam cover and get ready to install the lifters and lifter blocks. Step one is to oil the lifters and then slide them into the bores of the lifter blocks. To pre-lube the lifters Tony feeds oil in the hole in the center of the lifter (on top) with a small pump-style oil can, until oil comes out the hole in the side. Now the lifter block assemblies are set onto the engine, the rear one first, with a new

Not all pinion shafts are the same, this one uses a key for both the oil pump drive gear and the pinion gear, with a spacer in between. On the top right is the nut that keeps all the pieces in their place.

At this point the oil pump is assembled on the case. Note the two plugs in the top of the pump - these will be removed later for priming.

After installing the two gears and spacer the special nut is installed on the end of the shaft.

Breather end play is checked with a spacer on the end of the gear and a gasket in place.

Camshaft end play is checked with a feeler gauge (though a dial indicator can be used as well).

New lifters are coated with lube and dropped into the lifter blocks from the bottom.

gasket between block and case.

The small bolts are snugged down then torqued to 12 foot pounds (it's a good idea to check the service manual for all torque specifications). Before installing the cam cover for the last time Tony installs a new seal, using the correct driver. A little oil on the lip of the seal ensures the seal won't be damaged when the shaft begins to turn for the first time. Now the new outer gasket and cam cover can be installed for the last time.

With the cam and breather installed, Tony uses two hands to set the lifter blocks in place.

With a new seal installed, the cam cover is set into place for the last time.

Here we see the crank seal ready to be installed on the left side.

The cylinder is encouraged to slide over the rings while Tony exerts pressure against the bottom of the piston.

With both cylinders installed, Tony sets a new head gasket in place, then the heads themselves.

Though hard to see there's a new one-way valve on the upper right corner of the rocker box.

Before the cylinders and heads are installed the last item on the list for the bottom end is the installation of the crank seal on the engine's left side. Tony uses the correct driver and a few well placed whacks from a hammer to force the seal into place.

Cylinder Installation

Installation of the studs must occur before the cylinders themselves can be slipped into place. Tony applies red Loctite to the threads on each stud then screws them in with the help of a special head bolt, one with a ball bearing dropped down into the bolt's recess.

With the studs in place it's time to install pistons, rings and cylinders. First, however, Tony checks the end gap against the specification provided by S&S. This is a simple matter of sliding the two compression rings, one at a time, down into the cylinder and then checking the gap between the ends with a feeler gauge. Too little gap means the ends may butt together and cause ring distortion when the engine gets hot, too much means excessive blow-by of compression pressure.

Assured that the rings have the correct amount of end gap, Tony cleans up the bottom of the cases where the cylinders will sit to ensure a good seal. To make piston installation as simple as possible, the circlip is installed in one side of each piston, then

the rings are gently opened up with a special tool and set in place according to the instructions supplied with the ring set.

With lube on the piston pins and pin bosses, each piston is set over the connecting rod and the pin is pushed into place. After installing the pins Tony finishes up with the other circlip, making sure the clips snap into the groove in the bore of the piston.

Once the pistons and rings are in place Tony can coat the piston assemblies and the cylinders with a light film of oil and compress the rings prior to installation of the cylinders.

The ring compressor is equipped with a lock, so Tony can compress the rings, then use both hands to encourage the cylinder to slide down over the rings. The idea, of course, is that the cylinder forces the ring compressor out of the way as it slides down past the rings.

Before the heads are set in place Tony puts dowels in the heads and sets the head gaskets in place. Then it's time to set the cylinder heads on with a little oil on the threads and under the head-bolt washers. The bolts themselves are tightened to 40 pounds in ten-pound steps, following the sequence outlined in the service manual from Milwaukee.

The Arlen Ness rocker boxes use separate supports for the rocker arms...

The breather tube connects to either head with banjo bolts and then to the air cleaner.

..which are then installed into the lower section of the rocker box.

The carburetor being used in this engine is a S&S Super G, and Tony starts the installation by installing the intake manifold, after spraying a little silicone lube on the rubber compliance fittings.

The new billet rocker boxes come next and before setting the gasket in place Tony puts a little dab of Hylomar on the head surface. Now comes the gaskets and then the lower portion of these two-part rocker boxes. A look at the photo will show where Tony puts the little rubber umbrella valve just before the bottom section is set in place.

The bottom section of the rocker box is bolted on with five bolts (see the photo) before the pushrods, rocker arms and all the rest are installed.

Now the metal spacer and then the O-ring seals

must be installed in the lifter blocks. Before the pushrods and tubes can go in Tony must also put the correct O-rings in the base of the cylinder head where the push rod tubes push through.

Now Tony slides the pushrods down through the top of the head and through the pushrod tubes. These Crane pushrods come in two lengths. The longest are used on the outside, for the exhaust valves, while the two shorter pushrods are used inside. The Crane pushrods are preferred at Arlen's due to their slightly smaller diameter, which means they never hit the inside of the tubes like some others.

Tony turns the engine over, in the direction of rotation, until he has the rear cylinder ready to fire. This puts both cam lobes for the rear cylinder pointing down and the lifters on the base circle of the camshaft. After pre-lubing the support shafts, he installs the rocker arms and rocker arm supports, and tightens the support bolts.

To adjust the pushrods Tony sets them to zero lash, and then extends them "20 flats." As Tony explains, "the instructions say 18, but you always loose at least one flat when you lock them together." Tony goes through the same procedure for the rear cylinder, and then with the pushrods and rocker assemblies installed and adjusted for both cylinders Tony can extend the pushrod tubes and snap the clip into place.

With the valve train installed and the rocker box covers in place it's time to bolt the carburetor to the intake manifold. Once the carb is mounted to the intake with the thick insulator/gasket in place between the carb and intake, Tony can install the banjo fittings for the breather in either head and then clamp the hose to the banjo bolts with small tie wraps.

"I put the alternator on last," explains Tony. "The magnets make the engine want to stop at one specific spot, so it's hard to leave it at the best spot for adjusting the pushrods for example, so I leave it off until last." Installing the stator includes shoving the connector through the case, with a little silicon on the plug itself, and locking the stator itself in place with the four Allen bolts, each coated first with red Loctite. The final step in the alternator installation happens as Tony slips the magnet and washer in place on the shaft.

At this point the engine is essentially finished. What's left is to prime the oil pump and run the engine on the test stand.

Priming the pump consists of taking the two plugs out of the top of the oil pump, the tall one has a plunger underneath while the short one has a ball. Both must come out after the oil tank from the stand is hooked up. With the plugs out and the oil

lines hooded up Tony likes to make sure oil is working its way up both of the bores. When the oil has pushed all the air out of the bores Tone reinstalls the two plugs.

Tony explains that all the engines assembled at Arlen's are run before being shipped to be sure they run well, have good oil pressure and a good charging circuit.

"After priming the oil pump the engine should have oil pressure right away," explains Tony. "In fact, I like to crank the engine over without any ignition and make sure the oil pressure registers."

In this case the engine does show oil pressure while cranking and fires as soon as Tony turns on the ignition. Tony makes sure the charging circuit is working and then shuts the engine off to let it cool, before running it again to check for any oil leaks or possible problems.

The running check of oil pressure and voltage are noted on the check sheet and the complete engine is ready to ship.

Installation of the stator starts as Tony pushes the connector through the case, the small Allen bolt locks the plug in place.

Four Allen bolts hold the stator itself to the left side case.

Before shipping, each Arlen Ness engine is run on a test stand to ensure that it runs well, has good oil pressure and no leaks.

Section II - Chapter Seven

Hands-On: *Sequence #2*

ASSEMBLE TOP END AT DONNIE SMITH'S

For this sequence we follow along as Don Tima, resident engine guru at Donnie Smith Custom Cycles, assembles the top end of a 113 inch Evo-style V-Twin made up of components from TP Engineering.

For this particular sequence the bottom end is already assembled. Don is installing the pistons, cylinders, heads and camshaft. The engine is made up of all new components from TP Engineering. The flywheels are 4-1/2 inch 'wheels mated to four-inch bore cylinders and pistons from TP. The alternator is a 32 amp unit from The Motor Company. Ignition will be via a HI-4 assembly from Crane.

Prep and Paint Work

Even though these engines are available polished and assembled, Donnie Smith ordered this one in pieces primarily so the cylinders and heads could be painted. "When the heads and cylinders get here," explains Don Tima, "they're already polished. "But we need to paint them between the cylinders so the first thing we do is wash them good

The subject of this assembly sequence, 113 cubic inches of gleaming TP Engineering V-Twin as assembled by Don Tima at the shop of Donnie Smith.

with soap and water to get off the oily film, and then we glass-bead them so the paint will stick."

During the bead blasting and polishing operations Don and crew are careful with the details. "You have to be sure that you don't trap glass beads in the crack where the valve guide meets the head, we tape off this area with masking tape. And we also tape off the area on the head where the head bolts seat, so you don't torque down the bolts with paint under the head, because later the paint will turn to powder and you loose the clamping load."

Assemble the Heads

For this demonstration Don does a valve job, though that isn't usually necessary on the TP heads. Once the seats are cut he laps in the valves with water-soluble valve-lapping compound, explaining that "the water-soluble is much easier to clean up."

Assembling the heads begins with assembly lube on the valve stems before they are slipped up into the head. Next, Don installs the base for the spring, then the seals, which he installs with a dab of red Loctite (and the correct driver) and the warning that "You have to use extreme caution so you don't get Loctite on the stem or the stem will stick in the head." Now it's time to get out the spring compressor and install the springs and retainers. Don notes that the spring retainers should be evenly spaced with "cracks" of equal size on either side.

In this case the engine uses the recommended TP cam, so the TP heads were shipped with the correct springs i.e., springs with enough pressure to keep the valves on the lobes at higher RPM.

Rings and Pistons

Before installing the rings and pistons Don engages in another round of preparation work. Don likes to hone the cylinders, even though they were honed at TP, "because they've been handled so much they kind of loose the cross-hatch pattern, and this way I know the rings will seat with no trouble. This is a 280 grit ball hone, for finishing. It won't straighten out the bore, just leave the correct finish on the cylinder." Note: A hone like this is more often used to bust the glaze on used cylinders that won't be bored before the installation of new rings.

Once the cylinders are honed he washes them thoroughly with hot water and dish soap to get out

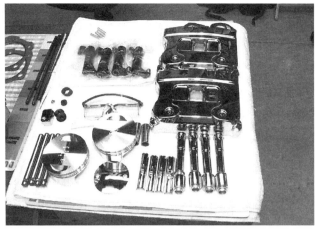

It's always a good idea to lay everything out ahead of time and check for missing parts or anything that was damaged in shipping.

Though the heads and cylinders were shipped "polished," they've been washed, bead blasted and painted before assembly.

Before the heads can be assembled Don does a valve job with the Neway cutters seen to the right of the heads.

As described in the Porting section, the valve job consists of cutting a wide 45 degree area which is narrowed with 30 and 60 degree cutters.

Laping in the valve shows Don exactly where the valve seals against the seat, and ensures a perfect seal between valve and seat.

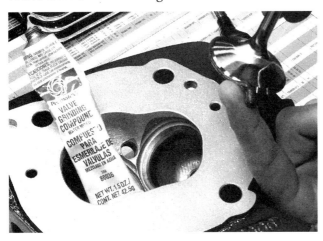

After the cutting is done Don applies valve grinding compound to the fact of the valve....

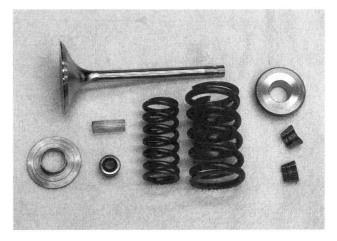

The springs, retainer and seal all came with the engine, so Don knows they are compatible with the camshaft.

.... then laps in the valve with some vigorous hand work.

A valve spring compressor is used to load the spring so Don can slip the valve spring retainers in place.

all the honing grit. It's important to use soap and water, as oil and solvents won't remove this material. After the wash job it's a good idea to coat the cylinders with oil or assembly lube to prevent any flash rust. Even the pistons get washed to eliminate any grit left from manufacturing.

Before the rings can be installed Don slides each of the compression rings down into the cylinder and checks the end gap. The biggest danger here is insufficient gap that might have the rings binding in the cylinder when the engine is hot. Specifications for end gap come with the rings, or can be found in the service manual.

With a ring expander Don installs the rings on the pistons, carefully following the recommendations for the top and bottom of each ring, and the recommended ring gap position that came with the ring set. Now that the cylinders are honed and the rings are on the pistons it's time to assemble the top end.

Once the rings are on the pistons Don installs eight carefully fabricated stud protectors on the cylinder studs and then applies liberal amounts of assembly lube to the rings and pistons. The piston pins are held in with a circlip on either end. Don has already installed the clip in one side of each piston. Now it's just a matter of positioning the piston down over the connecting rod, then inserting the piston pin, coated with lube, through the connecting rod and into the other side of the piston, followed by the missing circlip. Note: new circlips should be used anytime the pistons are replaced, they should never re-used.

Don explains that he likes assembly lube because it will stay in place longer than oil: "If this motor sits on the shelf for a year the oil film might break down. The assembly lube will be on there four years from now."

At this point Don rotates the flywheels so the front piston is near TDC. After installing the base gaskets and ensuring the ring gaps haven't changed from the ideal position, Don compresses the rings next, noting as he does: "It's important to realize that the compressor is installed 'upside down' as compared to an automotive engine so the top and bottom markings are wrong." With the rings compressed and a coating of lube in the cylinder Don

This is the ball hone used to create the cross-hatch pattern in the inside of the cylinders. Solvent is used as honing lubricant.

Soap and hot water are the only good way to get all the honing grit out of the cylinder. Without this step very rapid ring wear will result.

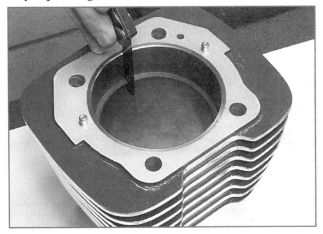

The ring gap is checked with a feeler gauge before the rings are installed on the pistons.

A piston ring expander (or snap-ring tool) is used to install the rings on the pistons. Rings are fairly brittle and easy to break.

Cylinder studs are wrapped with gas line so the pistons aren't nicked as the piston pin and the new circlip are installed.

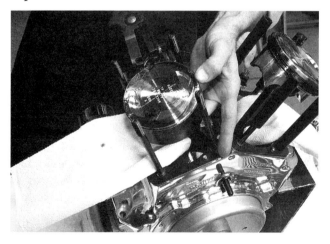

After rotating the piston rings so the gaps are positioned according to the manufacturer's directions, Don snaps the ring compressor in place.

A home made tool is used to lock the flywheels in place (with very little pressure on the flywheels) as Don raps the cylinder down over the piston rings.

removes the stud protectors and slides the cylinder down over the studs, encouraging it to slide down over the piston with raps from his open hand.

The head gaskets used here are composite gaskets, not the straight copper gaskets. Before screwing in the head bolts Don chases the threads and then oils them lightly to ensure the bolts screw down nice and easy on the studs.

Now Don tightens the head bolts to the specification given by S&S. Like all good mechanics Don tightens the bolts in stages, four in this case, following the tightening sequence provided by Harley-Davidson. Don doesn't do a formal re-torque of the bolts, but he does take a ten minute break before checking each of the head bolts with the torque wrench to make sure they haven't settled and loosened up.

With the head bolts torqued down Don can install the bottom of the rocker box assembly. "I like to glue some of the gaskets in place," explains Don, "like the gasket under the rocker boxes and the lifter blocks, then trim them after assembly. Because there's nothing worse than a piece of gasket hanging out after the motor is assembled."

Now it's time to install the bottom of the rocker box. But before going too far Don checks to make

The wire shows the corner where Don had to grind away metal to make room for the valve spring.

sure the valve springs clear the corner of the lower section of the rocker box assembly, A little grinding is sometimes necessary in this area (check the photos for clarification).

The lower section of the rocker box must be centered on the head. You can utilize two of the special tapered bolts designed to aid in positioning of the lifter blocks," explains Don, "or just move the box back and forth and make sure it's centered that way." Now it's time to install the three short 5/16 inch bolts in the base of the lifter box assembly, and the two Allen bolts at the corner. Don often puts the long 5/16 inch bolts (which will be tightened later) in their holes simply to keep the gasket correctly positioned.

Before installing the rocker arms and shafts, Don carefully puts assembly lube on the rocker shaft supports, the inside of the rockers and even the recess where the pushrod tip will fit. The rocker arms are roller-tip arms from *JIMS*. The installation of the pushrods and rockers is done one cylinder at a time and goes like this:

Crank the engine in the direction of rotation until you feel the intake lobe go well past it's peak. Now put a TDC indicator (like a plastic pen) in the spark plug hole. As the piston comes up toward TDC you know the engine is on the compression

Don tightens the head bolts to the specs from S&S in four stages. It's important that the torque wrench be in motion for the final reading setting.

Pre-lube is used in both the rocker supports...

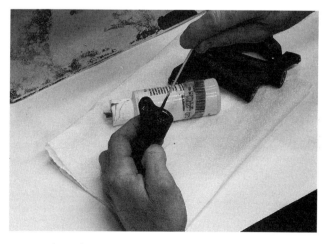

.... and in the inside of the roller rockers from JIMS.

1. Before the rocker shafts are set in place, Don slips the pushrods down from the head and through the collapsed pushrod tubes.

3. Now both valves on the rear cylinder can be adjusted. These lifters were not pumped up so there is no "bleed down" period.

4. The last part of the valve adjustment is to snap the push rod cover in place.

stroke (the intake stroke has just ended). At TDC both the intake and exhaust lobes are pointing down.

2. Once the push rods are in place Don can install the rocker arms and support shafts for the rear cylinder.

With the piston at TDC of the power stroke Don puts in both pushrods and the collapsed tubes, then the rocker arms and shafts. If the pushrods are two lengths, the longest are for the exhaust and the shorter ones are for the intakes. "You have to read what the pushrod manufacturer gives you for instructions," warns Don, "because each one adjusts differently depending on the thread pitch." Then Don marks the bottom of the pushrod and extends each one three full turns, plus one extra flat, "because you loose a little length when you jam the nuts together." With one cylinder done it's time to go through the same procedure for the other cylinder, and then extend the pushrod covers and snap the tube covers in place.

Before installing the center and top sections of the rocker boxes, Don lays out all the intake and carburetor parts. Each side of the intake is held in place with two Allen bolts. Don starts the bottom bolts for either side, positions the rectangular O-rings and flanges on either side of the intake, and sets the manifold assembly down into the V between the cylinders. The lower Allen bolts are tightened with a special ball-end Allen designed specifically for this purpose, while the upper bolts can be tightened with a conventional Allen wrench.

Once the intake bolts are tight, Don proceeds with the installation of the center and top section of the rocker boxes. For these assemblies Don likes the factory gaskets "because they fit really well and they don't squeeze out later."

Before setting the center rocker box sections in place, Don puts new umbrella valves into the hole on the left side of the D-ring (check the photos here).

With a sealer washer under the head of the Allen bolts Don tightens the rocker box top sections with a torque wrench. Next, Don installs two new spark plugs, being careful to first put anti-seize on the threads. At this point the engine is finished, minus only the carburetor and a double check to make sure nothing was overlooked during the assembly.

Note the new one-way umbrella valve in the top left of the rocker box, and the new factory gaskets being installed on either side of the D-ring.

All that's left now is the installation of the tops of the rocker boxes and the carburetor.

Hands-On: *Sequence #3*

QUICK AND DIRTY CAM INSTALLATION

In this cam installation the work is done *without* removing the heads. The work is done at Kokesh MC in Spring lake Park, Minnesota to a Heritage Softail. Jim Blesi starts by removing the points cover and then marking the position of the sensor plate. About cam installations in general, Jimmy feels it's always a good idea to replace the INA with a Torrington bearing, "they're only five dollars each," and that if the lifters have more than 10,000 miles on them it's a good idea to replace those too. For this type of installation, where there is no chance to check for valve-to-valve or valve-to-piston clearance, it's best to use a "bolt in" camshaft.

To rotate the engine Jimmy locks down the front wheel and jacks up the rear. With the spark plugs out he can easily rotate the engine by turning the rear wheel. Once the air cleaner is out of the way Jimmy collapses the pushrod covers and prepares to cut the pushrods with a hefty bolt cutter. It's not a good idea to use a die grinder for this as the grinding dust can go down into the engine.

Once the pushrods and tubes are out of the way Jimmy can go ahead and pull the lifter blocks. Next he removes the screws from the cam cover, installs a puller as shown, and pulls the cam cover - don't try to pry the cover off with two screwdrivers.

At this point it's a matter of removing one camshaft and replacing it with another, though as always there are a few tricks along the way. It's a good idea to inspect the breather gear for any signs of wear. Whether you use a plastic or metal gear, it should be installed with .001 to .011 inches of end play, (with a used gasket) checked as shown in the other, Arlen Ness, assembly sequence. You also have to be sure that both the new cam and the breather gear are timed correctly relative to the pinion gear.

Before the new cam is installed Jimmy checks the clearance between the inner-most cam lobe and the case. In some cases (pun intended) metal will have to be removed from the case with a small grinder. After pulling the old cam bearing a new Torrington bearing is coated with assembly lube and installed.

What makes this installation possible is the use

Disassembly starts with removal of the air cleaner and the sensor plate for the ignition.

After collapsing the push rod covers the deed is done with a huge bolt cutter.

This is the puller necessary for the removal of the cam cover.

The old camshaft is removed, along with the breather gear.

This is the area where aftermarket cams can hit the case. Zipper's makes a good tool for this.

Puller is used to remove inner cam bearing. Torrington bearing should be installed so wording faces out.

of the time-saver pushrods. Instead of dropping the pushrods down through the top Jimmy fully compresses the special pushrods (which compress to a shorter length) and slides the collapsed tubes over the pushrods. Then he slips the upper end of the pushrod into position in the recess in the rocker arm. While holding upward pressure on the pushrod he lines the bottom end up with the lifter. Now the pushrod is extended, with the cam turned so the lifter is sitting on the lowest part of the lobe, until it

fits loosely between the rocker arm and the lifter.

Adjustment, or how many turns from zero lash to fully adjusted, depends on the brand of pushrod and has been described elsewhere. Adjusting the valves on an engine that has been run recently is, however, different that performing the same operation on a new engine that has never been run – note the comments from Doug Coffee on page 126. What's left after the valve adjustment is to finish the re-assembly and set the timing.

This mock-up picture shows how a dial indicator can be used instead of a feeler gauge to check end play.

Special pushrods are fully collapsed, slipped up into the tubes and inserted from the bottom.

Valves are adjusted one cylinder at a time, leaving time for bleed down between (see Chapter Four).

Wolfgang Books On The Web

http://www.wolfgangpublications.com

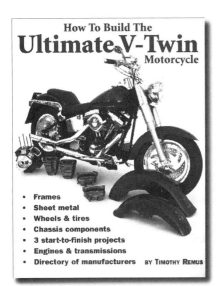

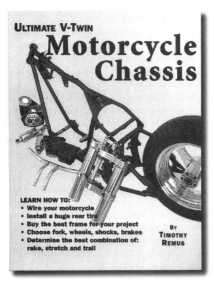

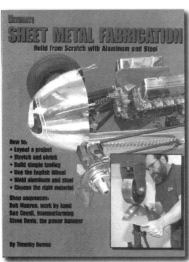

BUILD THE ULTIMATE V-TWIN MOTORCYCLE

10 chapters include:
- Build what's right for you
- Start with the right frame
- Use the best fork & suspension
- How much motor is enough
- Registration and insurance
- Paint or powder coat
- Sheet metal
- Assembly photo sequences

Publisher Tim Remus sought out the top custom bike builders to share their expertise with you. Hundreds of photos illustrate the extensive text. This is a revised edition with updated information and new products. If you're dreaming of the Ultimate V-Twin this is the place to start.

Ten Chapters   144 Pages $19.95

BUILD THE ULTIMATE V-TWIN CHASSIS

Ten chapters with 250+ photos.
- Frame buyers guide
- Which fork to buy
- Installing the driveline
- Sheet metal choices
- Powder coat or paint
- Mount a super wide rear tire
- How to pick the best brakes
- Understand motorcycle wiring

The foundation of any custom or scratch-built motorcycle is the frame. The look, ride and handling are all determined by the chassis. This book is part Buyer's Guide and part Assembly Manual. Shop Tours of Arlen Ness and M-C Specialties. Newly revised.

Ten Chapters   144 Pages $19.95

ULTIMATE SHEET METAL FABRICATION

Over 350 photos
11 chapters include:
- Layout a project
- Pick the right material
- Shrinkers & stretchers
- English wheel
- Make & use simple tooling
- Weld aluminum or steel
- Use hand and power tools

In an age when most products are made by the thousands, many yearn for the one-of-kind metal creation. Whether you're building or restoring a car, motorcycle, airplane or (you get the idea), you'll find the information you need to custom build your own parts from steel or aluminum.

Eleven Chapters   144 Pages $19.95

More Great Books From Wolfgang Publications!

http://www.wolfgangpublications.com

HOW TO: CUSTOM PAINT & GRAPHICS

Over 250 photos, 50% in color
7 chapters include:
• Shop tools and equipment
• Paint and materials
• Letter & pinstripe by hand
• Design and tapeouts
• Airbrushing
• Hands-on, Flames and signs
• Hands-on, Graphics

Seven Chapters   144 Pages

A joint effort of the master of custom painting, Jon Kosmoski and Tim Remus, this is the book for anyone who wants to try their hand at dressing up their street rod, truck or motorcycle with lettering, flames or exotic graphics. A great companion to Kustom Painting Secrets (below).

$24.95

KUSTOM PAINTING SECRETS

250 photos with color section
7 chapters include:
• History of House of Kolor
• How to Set up a shop
• Color painting sequences
• Prepare for paint
• Final paint application
• Hands-on, basic paint jobs
• Hands-on, beyond basic paint

Seven Chapters   128 Pages

• Hands-on, custom painting
More from the master! From the basics to advanced custom painting tricks, Jon Kosmoski shares his 30 years of experience in this book. Photos by publisher Tim Remus bring Jon's text to life. A must for ayone interested in the art of custom painting.

$19.95

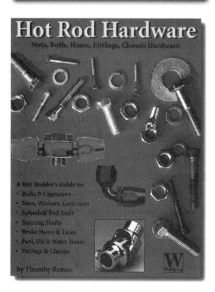

HOT ROD HARDWARE

Over 200 photos
9 chapters include:
• Why Hardware Matters
• Bolts & Capscrews
• Specialized Fasteners
• Nuts & Washers
• Torque Talk
• Plumbing
• Special Alloys

Nine Chapters   128 Pages

Understand the difference between a Grade 5 and a Grade 8 bolt, between a bolt and a capscrew. Know when to use - and not use - stainless bolts and nuts, or chrome instead of stainless. Understand the use of anti-seize and thread lockers. Know which type of lock nut is the best.

$19.95

Sources

Andrews Products
5212 Shapland Avenue
Rosemont, IL 60018
773/992-4014
www.andrewsproducts.com

Custom Chrome
1 Jacqueline Court
Morgan Hill, CA 95037
408/778-0500

Chrome Specialties Inc.
See your local CSI dealer
www.jammerclub.com

Compu-Fire
196 University Parkway
Pomona, CA 91768
909/598-5485
www.compufire.com

Crane Cams Inc.
530 Fentress Boulevard
Daytona Beach, FL 32114
904/252-1151
www.cranecams.com

Cycle Shack
See your local Cycle Shack dealer
www.cycle-shack.com

Delkron Manufacturing, Inc.
2430 Manning Street
Sacramento, CA 95815
916/921-9703

Donnie Smith Custom Cycles
10594 Raddison Rd NE
Blaine, MN 55449
612/786-6002

Dynatek
164 South Valencia Street
Glendora, CA 91741
626/963-1669
www.dynaonline.com

Dynojet Research
2191 Mendenhall Drive, Suite 105
North Las Vegas, NV 89031
702/399-1423
www.dynojet.com

Edelbrock
2700 California Street
Torrence, CA 90503
310/781-2222
www.edelbrock.com

Eagle Motor Company
4924 Para Dr.
Cincinnati, OH, 45237
513/242-7200

FLO Headworks
1150 Pike Lane #2
Oceano, CA 93445
805/481-6300

info@floheadworks.com

Harley-Davidson
See your local Harley-Davidson dealer

Head Quarters
6954 Glendon Drive
Melbourne, On Canada N0L 1T0
519/289-5229
www.head-quarters.com

Heavy Duty Cycles
2230 Kingston Road
Toronto, Canada M1N 1T9
416/265-1765
www.heavydutycycles.com

Hyperformance
5152A NE 12th Ave.
Pleasant Hill, IA 50317
515/266-6381

JIMS
See your local JIMS dealer
www.jimsusa.com

Johnson Engine Technologies
10 Springbrook Road
Westerly, RI 02891
401/596-9507

Lee's Speed Shop
1422 3rd Ave West
Shakopee, MN 55379
952/233-2782

Marquee Customs & Classics
72 Siemon Street
Bridgeport, CT 06605
203/332-1700

Mid-USA Cycle Parts
See your local Mid-USA dealer
www.mid-usa.com

Mikuni American
8910 Mikuni Avenue
Northridge, CA 91324

Ness, Arlen Inc.
16520 E 14th St.
San Leandro, CA 94578
510/276-3395

Rivera Engineering
12532 Lambert Rd
Whittier CA 90606
310/907-2600

S&S Cycle, Inc.
14025 County Highway G
Viola, WI 54664
608/627-1497
www.sscycle.com

Stamford Harley-Davidson and Buell
575-579 Pacific Street
Stamford, CT 06902

203/975-1985
www.hd-stamford.com

STD Development Corp.
10055 Canoga Avenue
Chatsworth, CA 91313
818/998-8226
www.stddevelopment.com

SuperTrapp Industries
4540 West 160th Street
Cleveland, OH 44135
216/265-8400
www.supertrapp.com

TP Engineering
5 Frances J Clarke Circle
Bethel, CT 06801
203/744-4960

Thunderheaders
Rich Products
12420 San Pablo Avenue
Richmond, CA 94805
510/234-7547

Trock Cycle Specialties
13N417 French Road
Hampshire, IL 60140
847/683-4010
trockcsi@aol.com

Vance & Hines
13861 Rosecrans Avenue
Santa Fe Springs, CA 90670
562/921-7461
www.vanceandhines.com

White Brothers
24845 Corbit Place
Yorba Linda, CA 92687
714/692-3404
www.whitebros.com

Wiseco Piston Inc.
7201 Industrial Park Blvd.
Mentor, OH 44060
440/951-6600
www.wiseco.com

Wood Performance
9835 Parkway East
Birmingham, AL 35215
205/854-8484
www.woodcarbs.com

Yost Power Tube
380 8th St NE
Milaca, MN 56353
320,/983-5410

Zipper's Performance Products
6655-A Amberton Drive
Elkridge, MD 21075
410/579-2100
www.zippersperformance.com